Menno in Athens

Menno in Athens: A Novel. A quirky charmer & unusual travel book & exploration of Greek myths and Christian origins via a young Mennonite.
Yikes, naked statues!

> —Margaret E. Atwood,
> on Twitter. July 29, 2022.
> (twitter.com/MargaretAtwood/status/1553121753093873664)

Imagine a young Menno, raised with a narrow cultural and doctrinal vision, whose eyes are opened to a wider world, revealing answers to questions he was told he shouldn't ask! Ronald Tiessen takes us on an intellectual pilgrimage through Hellenic culture, seen through an Anabaptist lens, offering a travelogue with an eye to questions of justice, equality, and violence in antiquity — all while gaining timeless insights into social ethics. The reader of *Menno in Athens* will sense the tensions which, in conversation with various companions, Menno tries to resolve between 'the gods' and his God, as known in his own faith tradition.

> — Jonathan Seiling
> Publisher, Gelassenheit Publications

An unlikely modern-day Odysseus, Menno is schooled in the religiosity and pacifism of his conservative rural community in Canada, yet finds himself on a memorable journey through contemporary Greece in search of the wisdom of the Ancients. To his surprise, encounters with an astonishing array of characters foreshadow fundamental norms of his sheltered home community, warn of disintegrating social and political life, and testify to the enduring folly of war that delivers only defeat to victors and vanquished alike. *Menno in Athens* is a unique, compelling journey of discovery, and the reader's good fortune is to be along for the ride.

> — Ernie Regehr
> Senior Fellow in Defence and Arctic Security at the Simons Foundation Canada, and Research Fellow in the Centre for Peace Advancement at Conrad Grebel University College, University of Waterloo.

This rich and provocative work is not so much a novel in the usual sense but a kind of literary Rubik's Cube: part philosophical essay, part spiritual reflection, and part travelogue. For me, it is in the last of these aspects that the story finds its greatest and most satisfying impact: as a journey, as an exploration, across centuries and continents... deep into the meaning of myth and religion and poetry; into the inspirations of Greece then and now; and perhaps above all into the persistent compulsions of a young man to know the path that has led him to where he is, and that he must now extend forward into a more resilient and personal understanding of the world and of himself.

> — Charles Wilkins is the author of fifteen books, including *The Circus at the Edge of the Earth* (McClelland & Stewart, 1999), *In the Land of Long Fingernails* (Penguin, 2009), and the international bestseller, *Paddle to the Amazon* (McClelland & Stewart, 1987).

This enthralling novel takes us on what might at first seem to be a quixotic pilgrimage to the sites of ancient Greece to validate a vision of how free people can live, and thrive, in harmony – a vision that two thousand years later found an echo among Anabaptist Mennonites. When the hero, aptly named Menno, leaves the Mennonite town where he grew up (sometime in the 1970s), he is strenuously warned by his stepfather that he is pursuing false gods.

Menno has the ardour and passion of youth, but he is by no means naïve. He is already well versed in the history and literature of ancient Greece. In fact, it is his stepfather who has a naïve schoolboy image of incessantly warring Greek tribes, recounted in gory detail in their poetry, drama, and sculpture. What Menno validates on his pilgrimage is their scorn, not their celebration, of private wealth and martial glory. For a brief period, during the sixth and fifth centuries BC, they created that rare thing, a *polis* – small, radically democratic enclaves in the midst of warring kingdoms and empires, that recognized no earthly hierarchy or authority other than their own impassioned searching to discern what constitutes a just and truly rich life. And what else but a *polis* were those agrarian Mennonite settlements—whether in Russia, Paraguay, or Canada—where they too aspired to live an exemplary life that was pleasing to God?

> — Erwin Wiens, retried professor of English Literature, and author of *To Antoine: A Novel* (Gelassenheit Publications, 2022).

Menno in Athens

A Novel

by

Ronald Tiessen

with cover artwork and sketches by

Lisa Rollo Kipp

PANDORA
PRESS

Library and Archives Canada
Cataloguing in Publication

Title: Menno in Athens : a novel /
by Ronald Tiessen;
with cover artwork and sketches by Lisa Rollo Kipp.
Names: Tiessen, Ronald, author.
Description: Includes bibliographical references.
Identifiers: Canadiana 20220403074 |
ISBN 9781926599748 (softcover)
Subjects: LCGFT: Novels.
Classification: LCC PS8639.I365 M46 2022 |
DDC C813/.6—dc23

Ebook ISBN-13: 978-1-926599-96-0
Hardcover ISBN-13: 978-1-926599-97-7

Author: Ron Tiessen
Book cover image and sketches by Lisa Rollo Kipp
Book design and editing by Maxwell Kennel
Pandora Press logo and illustration design by Jonathan Dyck

Menno in Athens is a work of fiction, and all the characters are imaginary, with the exception of Bishop Irenios, H.D.F. Kitto, J. Winfield Fretz, Henry Pauls, and Simone Weil.

MENNO IN ATHENS
ISBN: 978-1-926599-74-8

Copyright © 2022 Pandora Press

Published by Pandora Press
All rights reserved.

www.pandorapress.com

In memory of my parents
John and Margaret Tiessen
with gratitude

—

for my grandsons
Charlie and Max
with love

Acknowledgments

For inspiration and guidance during my student years I am grateful to J. Winfield Fretz and Walter Klaassen at Conrad Grebel College, Professor Dimitris Nianias and H.D.F. Kitto in Athens, and to Simone Weil whose spell was cast from the opposite shore of the River Styx.

I am thankful to island neighbours, Lisa Rollo Kipp and Lois Armstrong, for their contributions. For their trust and invaluable professional advice, I am indebted to Jonathan Seiling, John Rempel, and Erwin Wiens, who bear no responsibility for distortions, and for the abiding support of my wife, Kathryn.

Finally, I am indebted to Maxwell Kennel of Pandora Press for both moral and additional indispensable support.

Table of Contents

Foreword

The Pilgrimage

> Olympia
> Pharsala
> Athens Ancient Agora
> Mykonos
> Paros
> Rhodes-Lindos
> Karpathos-Tristomo
> Kos
> Bodrum-Halicarnassos
> (Turkey)
> Miletos
> Priene
> Lesbos
> Mytilini
> Eressos
> Chios
> Samos-Pythagorio
> Thebes
> Sparta
> Epidauros
> Troezen
> Poros
> Milos
> Eleusis
> Athens: Theatre of Dionysos
> Ancient Agora
> Acropolis

Postscript, Notes, and Menno's Reading List

Foreword

It was a dream of mine to return to Greece after studying in Athens. It would be a pilgrimage should the dream come true. And so, it did. This account — *Menno in Athens* — describes that pilgrimage and travel adventure, albeit one of a contemplative bent. Its subject touches upon a nascent face of Christianity – one not always recognized in its so-called 'pagan' context. In my travels, narrated below, I do not address the organized religions of our day unless they concern an early chapter in religious history. Instead, this account embraces the voices of teachers, sages, poets, playwrights, and philosophers from a time long before the birth of Jesus of Nazareth.

I assume that enquiry and the pursuit of truth should know no boundaries, as was once the case in archaic and classical Greece, when natural philosophy and religion were indivisible. The thought of this time, as revealed through literature and mythology, is the centrepiece of the musings that follow.

Ancient Greece warrants this honour for several reasons. Firstly, ancient Greeks were both curious and receptive to new ideas. The figure of Aphrodite is an example of ancient Greek openness in her acceptance at Olympia as a goddess of love, now daughter of Zeus. She appeared as an earlier goddess of love, Astarte, from Syria-Canaan. The Greeks' penchant for trade and travel also fed their curiosity. Solon received an audience at Sais with Pharaoh Amasis II, and Solon visited King Croesus of Lydia at Sardis. Lycurgus too received inspiration for his Spartan code of law from Crete (possibly the codification at Gortyn?) and Egypt.

Trade with the Phoenicians resulted in a significant evolution of the Greek alphabet, and much more. It opened a door to outside influences during the early archaic period: sculpture and vases in particular, provide expression of the hybridization of animals like griffins and sphinxes. Decorative styles and motifs like palmettes, rosettes, and lotuses appeared. Throughout these years, Athens welcomed outsiders with their new ideas and reports from abroad.

Yet, they never failed to put their stamp on what they borrowed: the sculptural masterpieces that evolved from the stiff Egyptian kouroi; the Hittite chimaera that once warded off evil became the chimaera conquered by Bellerophon. Moreover, their geographical location acted as a funnel that directed ideas and discoveries from two continents. This was borne out in a wide range of subjects from sacred matters to literature from the Sumerians, mathematics from the Babylonians, and medicine from Egypt. It was significant too that the gifts received from these cultures came from much older civilizations, like Sumeria, Egypt, and perhaps even India.

Secondly, the ancient Greeks were not hampered by dogma as we know it; nor by a rigid religious hierarchy; nor by a single written source of authority. This allowed playwrights, for example, to understand myths through their own mind's eye, which in turn led to greater openness in their pursuit of truth.

Thirdly, and as compellingly, the Greeks had no singular word for religion – a fact that may suggest that one is left to define religion for oneself, or perhaps more accurately, that religion is coterminous with life itself. What is certain is that any subject that even skirts the subject of religion will be daunting, and no less so in our time. ΙΧΘΥΣ is the ancient Greek word for fish. As early as the first century Christians employed the term as an acronym, or acrostic, for Ιησους Χριστος, Θεου Υιος, Σωτηρ, Jesus Christ, Son of God, Saviour. A slippery subject indeed. Of course, it must be added that the Gospels were written in Greek, and language necessarily comes out of a culture, with an appendage of etymology, of precedent, and memory.

While Menno only had a rudimentary grasp of ancient Greek, he recalled an instructor who said that if languages were thought of as a tree, some fluttered about the top branches, while ancient Greek was found down in the roots of the tree. Here images arose to fashion meaning – a place where words were born.

The pilgrimage that is documented here comes from a contemporary by the name of Menno. His meanderings through Greece take place in the 1970s. Menno is a bit of an eccentric fellow, not the least for his interest in what stands at the beginning of what we now call Christianity. In terms of interests, he is not your average person. However, to Menno's mind — and very much in keeping with his habit of returning to the early church for guidance — origins were as important as anything else humanity touches, whether it be democracy or religion. Moreover, Menno was aware that, for some, Greek and Christian thought were understood to be inherently opposed — a view which he felt had not enjoyed adequate questioning. It was a view that did not consider the open discussion and debate characteristic of the first two centuries, nor did it acknowledge the training in Greek philosophy enjoyed by several of the early church fathers.

Menno inherited by birth and education a way of looking at the world that originated in 16th century Switzerland and the Netherlands. This interpretation of Christianity was both Catholic and Protestant, and it was given the name 'Anabaptism' because followers practiced adult (re)baptism as an entry into the community of believers. Menno was named after a leader of the Anabaptists in the Netherlands, Menno Simons.

Over time those of a similar stripe as Menno came to be known as *Menniste*, or Mennonites. Firmly appended to his inheritance, and as a result of his studies, Menno nurtured an interest in and fondness for Athens, the 'school of Hellas'. He also perceived continuities between certain voices within ancient Greek culture and his own faith background. On a broad canvas there were some remarkable and often overlooked parallels: a divine parent to explain 'superhuman' lives, the occurrence of resurrection, the long tradition of healing, the role of asceticism, the despair of violence, and the desperate need for love.

Menno directed his attention to voices from a small number of the hundreds of ancient Greek city-states. To some degree, these characterized the archaic and early classical periods of antiquity and came from the body of literature that has somehow miraculously survived until our day. When the stories could be traced to a specific place, Menno's goal was to visit the place. In the spirit of the second century CE traveller Pausanias, Menno journeyed throughout Greece in the hope that being present at the site would be an inspiration, and would perhaps reveal more. His guides reappeared to provide assistance, from as early as Homer in the 8th century BCE to Pausanias. In his approach, Menno was influenced by the example set by the fifth century BCE historian Herodotus. He aspired to be as curious as the historian, but he also sought synchronicity between apparently disparate cultures.

A word about how it all began: as Menno gave it some thought, he found that the answer lay in books that he had discovered in the library. Menno read *The Greek Way* and the *Echo of Greece* a few years before he studied in Athens. These were written by the renowned classicist Edith Hamilton. Through this portal of Victorian vantage, Menno was drawn into a particular representation of the ancient Greek world. The *Dialogues of Plato*, *The Greek Experience* by C. M. Bowra, and the tragedies of Aeschylus only strengthened the allure.

Menno's stepfather, Paeta became quite upset when he found such reading material in his house. Such books belonged to the pagan world, and not in their family home. To challenge Paeta was futile. During these moments of friction, Menno's mother was quiet, but appeared overcome with sadness. Before Menno left to study in Athens, Paeta lost his composure. He had seen pictures of the naked Greek sculptures, and the icons that filled Greek churches! In fairness, Paeta was not the only problem. Menno's father had died three years earlier and had been a respected leading minister in their home church. He would have been disappointed in Menno's plans, but tolerant, nonetheless. There were also other voices of discouragement. Menno had first majored in Religious Studies and Anabaptist and Reformation History, but he had changed his focus to Archaic Greek Literature in the last two years of his studies. At that time, there were pressing family expectations, particularly those of his grandmother, that he would go on to study at a seminary.

But Menno persevered in his interests and went on to study in Athens. The enticement of ancient Greece grew as that world was opened to him. After his second year he felt an urge to stay in Greece. He even applied for a Teaching Assistant position at an American college in Athens. It would take some time before the outcome of the competition was announced. In the meantime, he would visit his family.

After returning to Canada, he soon slipped into comfortable routines of family, old friendships, and church life. Until, that is, he received a letter from Athens — good news that something would be made to work for him. He could study and work with two professors, one teaching Early Greek Literature, the other Ancient Greek Religion. His family was told about the opportunity to continue his studies in Greece, but not any details like the dream-like match with his interests. He had six weeks to accept the offer.

For the present, Menno had to deal with the apparent rift between his past and his love for ancient Greek civilization. Menno was quite aware that he belonged to the Anabaptist tradition, but also that Greece held an inexplicable attraction for him. He was taught that one could not serve two masters. But he wanted to believe that there might be just one master, perceived as having two faces. Moreover, Menno could not fully understand himself, let alone explain to others, what the allure was that ancient Greece represented for him — one so foreign and removed in time. He wondered about reincarnation, and whether in a previous life he had not sailed the wine dark sea and breathed the air beneath the Greek sun. Altogether this was not quite the road to Damascus, but a fork in the road lay before Menno nonetheless, and perhaps also a shift in how he would look upon the world.

When he announced his decision to return to Athens, Menno's mother was in tears, for she knew the separation that would follow. It was just so far away. And Paeta would not yield. He began,

'I want to be clear on where you are going with your ancient Greeks. I suppose that you are suggesting the Greeks are the chosen people?'

Menno replied with some caution because he feared Paeta would make him say things he was unprepared to discuss, let alone reveal.

'No, the Greeks would not have considered themselves a chosen people. They were quite aware of their indebtedness to older neighbouring civilizations. The story of Greece was one of borrowing ideas and being colonized by people from Phoenicia and Egypt, as illustrated by Cadmus and Nauplios respectively.

The Greeks saw themselves differently. For one, their government, called a democracy, did not copy that of their neighbours. The administration of their city-state was in the hands of the many, rather than the few. This meant that their statecraft concerned itself with justice for all citizens. Isonomia, equality before the law, was intended to be common to all.

In time, this impulse toward equality came to define the city-state. What followed was an understanding of freedom that was characterized by participation in political decisions and activities. The distinct difference was that no one ruled singularly over others. Herodotus succinctly summarized the communal place of law and equality when asked by the Persian Queen Atossa what master the Greeks obey. He answered, 'they have no masters, they obey the laws.'

Paeta interrupted Menno, saying: 'This business of government is of no interest to me.'

'The prophecy of the Messiah in the Old Testament; is that not central to our understanding of the fulfillment in the Gospels? You seem to be deviating from what is at the heart of our beliefs. Next I imagine you will be starting your own church with its own commandments and creed!'

Menno hesitated before responding.

'I fear that you do not recognize the similarities between our Mennonite participatory model of governance within the congregation and Greek democracy.'

'I am not denying the importance of prophecy in the Scriptures. However, I am raising the question of whether stories in another culture might not have prefigured the life of Jesus of Nazareth. Prometheus, who suffered for giving humankind understanding, may have been one such figure. And was not Jesus also viewed as a teacher by his disciples? What if you discover similar teachings among the Greeks before the time of Christ? The Greek myths are not merely untrue stories. Myths reflect a culture's deepest values and aspirations, and in so doing they are conveyors of meaning, sometimes so full of meaning that we live and die by them. It seems to me that sometimes stories which appear implausible can be indicative of another order of truth.'

Paeta interjected, 'I imagine you even consider your Greek myths to be divine revelation! Everything you say points to a denial of the true revelation in Scripture.'

Menno replied somewhat hastily, 'Paeta, if you have the proclamation of a truth in one case that is considered divine revelation, and the exact same proclamation found in another culture or by another name, must we assume one is divinely inspired and the other not? Moreover, in ancient Greece when poets and bards composed and sang, it was taken for granted that they were inspired by the presence of one of the Muses, a daughter of Zeus. A being from beyond was commonly acknowledged as granting the artist his or her voice. For example, the *Iliad* begins, in the Lattimore translation: 'Sing, goddess, the anger of Peleus' son Achilleus and its devastation…'

Paeta, the precedent for understanding supernatural figures as an offspring of a god and mortal is widespread in ancient Greece.

Apollo is the father of Orpheus and Asklepios, Heracles and Perseus are sons of Zeus, Bellerophon and Theseus are offspring of Poseidon, Harmonia is the daughter of Ares and Aphrodite, to mention but a few of the examples of dozens that pervade the landscape of Greek mythology. All share in one thing: their exceptionality cannot be explained in any other way but by their parentage.

In some cases, resurrection was featured as an exceptional feat. As it was vital to the Gospel's good news, so it was in the stories of those in ancient Greece, where a human being was singled out and lifted beyond common mortals. In contrast to the very few examples from the Old Testament – in Kings for example – in ancient Greece many mortals made the journey to Hades, and back! Among well know figures are Orpheus, Odysseus, Aeneas, Heracles, Theseus, Asklepios, Persephone daughter of Demeter, Hippolytus son of Poseidon, and Er mentioned in Plato's *Republic*.'

Menno continued,

'Paeta, I certainly do not have all the answers, but I feel somewhat more at home within the first two centuries after the resurrection, when interpretation of what it all meant was varied, when the canon of the New Testament was not yet set, and when creeds and sources of authority were hotly discussed and debated. This temporarily inclusive circumstance lasted for a few centuries. It was a fluid religious landscape, one of jostling ideas, and one in which the Gospel of John could proclaim the pre-existence of the Logos; the Logos that would be made flesh. I guess I am left wondering what that could mean, and whether this pre-existence could be detected in ancient Greece.

I wish to continue learning about 'my Greeks,' as you call them, but I have no intent to denigrate my Mennonite heritage. Rather, I am drawn in by the sense of familiarity I experience when studying the thought of the ancient Greeks. It's as though the Mennonites of today and the ancient Greeks share some common ground, and even some salient insights. Did not several of the early church fathers themselves sense this foreshadowing of their new faith? Besides, for me the Truth of the Gospels is not threatened by earlier epiphanies. In fact, earlier visions can even serve to underpin revelation in Scripture. I do not aim to go against your will, but there is simply too much that fascinates me to change course. With regret, for the time being we have to accept that you and I will disagree.'

Paeta spoke further, saying to Menno: "If you persist in holding these views, you are right, we will not find agreement. I have to admit I have agonized over how you have come to this unfortunate way of thinking. Is what you have read the problem? I doubt that I would understand you any better if I knew; nevertheless, why could you not let me have a look at some of these books?"

Menno could not bring a pile of books along on his pilgrimage. He had made notes and copied excerpts from several publications to read at various stops.

These came from a carefully selected list of books, many of which were sources of his inspiration. Why not hand over the list to Paeta, he thought. It was highly unlikely that he would even read them, particularly if the list proved daunting for its length. And thus Paeta came into possession of the list of books sacred to Menno.

But Menno now wished he had said nothing, and Paeta managed his raw feelings, saying that he would pray for Menno. There was no mention of a pilgrimage, but the plan was fully formed in Menno's mind. Before leaving, Paeta asked for contacts and places where he could be reached. Menno obliged, even though he felt uneasy about it. Did Paeta have something up his sleeve?

'Yet patience — there shall come

Many great voices from life's outer sea,

Hours of strange triumph,
and when few men heed,

Murmurs and glimpses of eternity.'

—Excerpt from *Outlook* by Archibald Lampman
from his memorial cairn, Morpeth, Ontario

The Pilgrimage

Temple of Hera, Olympia

Olympia

Menno was reading Thucydides at the time he arrived in Athens. In Book V (5:43) the historian wrote of how the Spartans had been banned from participating in the games at Olympia. He wrote that the Lakedaimonians (Spartans) had attacked a fortress of Elis during the truce. Menno wondered what this truce was all about. He also recalled a passage in Herodotus in which he described the Persian King Xerxes' introduction to the games of the Greeks. He learned that the Greeks contended not for money but for an olive wreath. Xerxes expressed his astonishment to his general Mardonius, as to what sort of people they had come to fight, men who competed for honour more than other rewards!

On the next day Menno departed by bus through bucolic countryside from Athens via Tripolis to the site of ancient Olympia. Upon arrival he entered the archaeological site and chose a seat on the opisthodomos (west end) of the Temple of Zeus. Here Herodotus is thought by Lucian to have read from his *Histories*. The seat offered a direct view of the accommodations called the Leonidaeon on the south, Phidias' workshop across the way, and the Palaestra to the north. From Pausanias he learned that in the prolonged conflict between Pisa and Elis, women of good reputation were selected from sixteen of the cities under the control of Elis, and these peacemakers settled the longstanding grievances between them. The same women were put in charge of weaving Hera's robe and organizing the first games at Olympia, in honour of Hera.

Menno had had no idea that the celebrated games were begun by women, and that the women were selected to arbitrate an end to the long-lived conflict of the city-states. He was surprised to learn that the Games were in honour of Hera, not Zeus, and that peacemaking was so prominent in its origins.

He also learned that the athletic contests were held every four years, beginning in 776 BCE. They were organized locally and were in the earliest years regional in extent, becoming pan-hellenic as they gained renown. As the Games came to include Greeks from the Black Sea and Asia Minor, and all the way to Libya in North Africa and Sicily in the West, their importance was symbolized by the Greeks' adoption of the Games as a measure of time: for example, as an event having occurred in the 72nd Olympiad.

The Games were competitions to honour victors, but they were also more than that. They were conducted to celebrate the commonality of Greeks across hundreds of city-states. Theirs was a complex shared heritage: of song, language, poetry, heroes, myths and of course, shared gods. Many Greeks who visited Olympia and gazed at the pediment sculpture on the fifth century BCE Temple of Zeus, would have understood that Apollo was bringing resolution to the conflict between Lapiths and Centaurs at the famed wedding of Pirithous. Much as every Anabaptist would recognize the etching by Jan Luyken featured on the cover of the 1660 Dutch publication, *The Martyrs' Mirror* by Thieleman J. van Braght. In the depiction

Dirk Willems saves the life of a man who is pursuing him and who has fallen through the ice – the man who would return him to prison and a martyr's death. The sixteenth century Anabaptists and many contemporary Mennonites believe that Dirk's faith called for him to save another's life, even if it meant losing his own.

In celebrating commonality, the Games were also to lead toward a cessation of hostilities among the city-states. To accomplish this a sacred truce for the games was agreed upon as recorded on the disc of Iphitus and seen by Pausanias. It may have dated from about a hundred years before the official inauguration of the games. Some allege that it began as a treaty signed between Iphitus of Elis, Lycurgus of Sparta, and Kleosthenes of Pisa. For three months, the territory of Olympia was inviolable. The treaty ensured the safety of athletes and pilgrims making their way to and from the competitions. No armed persons were allowed entry into the territory of Elis. It was viewed as sacrilege to do so.

When the Spartans violated the truce in 420 BCE they were prohibited from making sacrifices to the gods at Olympia. In addition, they were fined 200,000 drachmas (a daily wage at the time for a craftsman was about one drachma). The breaking of trust in the Sacred Truce was viewed as a serious matter and came with a severe penalty.

For three months, the normal incessant hostilities between states were to cease. Greeks were to live in concord. Indeed, the name given the Sacred Truce was 'εκεχειρία,' which meant a holding of hands. It proved an endorsement of a moment of peacefulness in an otherwise violent world, in which Greek city-states were almost constantly at war with one another. This world was described in Aristophanes' play Lysistrata (l.1131) as one with 'Greeks destroying Greek men and cities, while worshipping the same gods at common altars, like those at Olympia.'

The spondophoroi were appointed officials who were in charge of the Sacred Truce. Menno recalled that the σπονδοφόροι were the ones who brought proposals for a truce, while σπονδή is the libation made in concluding treaties. Ειρήνη, for peace, was in use in antiquity, but not in this context. As such, they enjoyed recognition and prestige as peacekeepers. Consequently, they were invited to mediate peace treaties in other places beyond Olympia. Menno found these peacekeeping efforts to be surprisingly resonant with his heritage, almost like a counter-current to the prevailing glorification of heroes on the battlefield. Why had not the peacemaking aspect of the Games been continued? Menno wondered if he was misinterpreting the centrality of the Sacred Truce.

Before leaving Olympia, Menno had to visit the unusually rich collection at the Archaeological Museum. There were so many exceptional sculpture masterpieces, from the pediment sculpture and the metopes on the Temple of Zeus depicting the labours of Heracles, to the Hermes statue by Praxiteles, the Nike by Paionios, and the rare surviving head of the cult statue of Hera found in her temple in the temenos.

Pharsala

Pharsala, Thessaly

The games and the Truce here in Olympia brought to mind the earlier games described in Homer's *Iliad*. In both cases an oasis of concord was fashioned, which represented a treasured exception in a vast desert of discord. With great regret, Menno was unable to get to the site of Troy in present day Turkey. His alternative was to visit Thessaly. To do so he had to return to Athens and transfer to the bus line going north. His destination was Pharsala, between Karditsa and Volos. In the Mycenaean period, the Homeric Phthia is thought to have been located somewhere about here. Menno found his way up a dirt track that led to the summit of Mount Prophetis Elias. At the top were sections of cyclopean walls from the bronze age, a gate entrance to the north, and a possible site of Peleus' palace where Achilles would have been raised. This may have been a good deal of conjecture on Menno's part, as archaeological work was yet required to confirm all of this – that this site was home to the kingdom of Peleus, the warrior Myrmidons who fought as part of the Achaean allies, and the home of Achilles and his friend from childhood, Patroclus.

Menno was surprised to meet a hiker at this remote site. He introduced himself as someone who had spent some time in the region, almost twenty years ago. His name was Virgil and he had taken some brief holidays near Volos when working for PAX-MCC (Mennonite Central Committee). He explained that he had been a volunteer and conscientious objector, but had arrived in northern Greece, at Panayitsa, in 1953. He was a dairy adviser and was brought to Panayitsa at a time after the civil war in Greece when much of the country had been left impoverished. He had made a number of contacts and friends at the American Farm School outside of Thessalonica. That Menno would encounter this stranger who belonged to the Mennonite world was even more astonishing. Small world. Virgil had shared who he was and seemed an amicable fellow. It may have been for that reason that Menno told Virgil why he was at this site, and why he felt free to share his views on the funeral games in the *Iliad*.

He explained that near the end of a decade of war with the Trojans, Book XXIII of the *Iliad* gives the account of the death of Patroclus. As he was not just a comrade-at-arms, but the closest of friends and 'θεράπων', who at the time of his death happened to be wearing Achilles' armour, it was as though he sacrificed himself for his friend. Unsurprisingly, Homer dedicates a lengthy account to the funeral games of the hero.

The backdrop to the games is, of course, the ongoing war: death, destruction, and never-ending suffering, brought about by the conflict being played out on the Trojan Plain and beyond. The suffering bled beyond the battlefield. Portraits of the dying reveal the loss felt far away: a grandfather left with no one to care for him, a child left fatherless, a wife abandoned and destined for slavery. Nor does Homer spare his audience the graphic images of a warrior's bowels spilling onto the dust, of brains spattered onto fellow warriors, of shattered teeth, of the precise course taken by a spear, on its way through the human anatomy, of moaning and agony all around.

And into this depiction Homer inserts the account of the funeral games for Patroclus. The contrapuntal effect is immediate. The world of battle has been left behind, except for reminders that underline its contrast with peacetime. The first event, that of the chariot race, at once sets the stage for otherness. Achilles pities Eumelos who could not finish the race because the goddess Athena had smashed his chariot. Achilles awards him a prize nonetheless, a breastplate. Antilochus wins second prize after cutting off Menelaus. The latter objects that Antilochus should win the prize mare. He insists that the younger Antilochus swear an oath by the gods that he did not play foul. Antilochus backs down, bending his heart, and gives the mare to Menelaus, who in turn offers it back. In addition, Achilles' magnanimity ensures that old King Nestor, who did not even compete, should receive a prize as well.

This first event mediates to accomplish concord. There is reverence and generosity. The warriors treat one another more as equals, as in the third contest, that of wrestling. Here Achilles declares a draw between Odysseus and Ajax, who will share the prizes.

In spear casting, the prize goes without a contest to King Agamemnon. He is the best after all. And in this gesture, Homer's audience is expected to recall the earlier heightened antipathy between Achilles and Agamemnon. Altogether, these games represent a separate domain from war. In this world, mercy is shown, forgiveness is offered, magnanimity is demonstrated, and violence is aborted. Standing at variance with the scene of battle is the attempt to live in harmony, something not at all to be expected, even among those joined in opposition to a common enemy.

For Menno, this was an intimation of the 'βασιλεία των ουρανών,' the kingdom of the heavens, a realm with consciousness of stark difference. It happens that in ancient Greece it was customary to find a stadium for athletic competitions at sacred sites, as the games were an integral part of what we might loosely term 'worship.'

Virgil had a fondness for the Greek people, he admitted. Yet, Menno got an earful in response to his interpretation of the ancient world and their funeral games. Even though it was a great epic poem, for Virgil the *Iliad* was nonetheless a made-up story. It was fiction and myth; not to be taken seriously. And the business of the games being understood as the kingdom of heaven was a 'stretch,' at the very least. Virgil went on for some time, while dismissing the meaningfulness of mere games and questioning how one could find the kingdom of heaven in a setting of violent competitions. Menno forgave him because his response was to be expected, given his background. However, Virgil also had a child-like curiosity and seemed truly interested in why Menno was on this journey – and he always had that twinkle in his eye. The fellow was amicable by nature, and before departing he asked Menno where he was headed after Pharsala, as though he were genuinely interested. They wished each other 'καλό ταξίδι' and went their separate ways.

Menno left Thessaly enamoured with the role the games played at Olympia and on the Trojan plain, where men could vie for honour and glory without engaging in battle. The games demarcated a separate place and attitude where friendship was celebrated in feisty competitions, in place of a bloody victory over one's enemy. Albeit, that athletic competitions should be seen as an integral part of the worship of the gods, that the games invited comparison with the 'kingdom of the heavens', would be hard to digest by Anabaptists, as Menno had just witnessed. As a result, Menno could not help but continue to entertain doubt. Perhaps others' objections would be diminished if reminded that the outcome aborted strife and celebrated the oneness of Greeks.

Ancient Agora Athens

Ostraca, The Archaeological Museum of the Athens Agora

Upon Menno's return to Athens, he visited the Agora Museum of the American School of Classical Studies. The Agora was the marketplace where citizens assembled to gossip, discuss politics, business, and subjects pertaining to philosophy. It was the site of the inner workings of democracy in the city-state. The Greek Archaeological Society had begun excavations in the 19th century, and these were continued in earnest with a major infusion of financial support from the Rockefellers in 1931. The findings across the excavation were stunning.

Menno had read about the Athenian practice of choosing public officials by sortition, that is, by lot. The practice included magistrates and archons, as well as jury members in the courts, alongside the five hundred members of the Boule, or senate. The method of filling the roles of government reminded Menno of his own faith community that once chose ministers by lot. It was a tradition that side-stepped expertise and allowed for greater participation of members. It was, at the same time, a vote of confidence for egalitarianism. And the question remained whether this practice allowed room for the intervention of the gods in the affairs of the city-state, as was the case for those cultures that sought divine approval in selecting leaders for the faith community.

In the museum, Menno found the mechanism used for the selection of people by lot. There were bronze tokens used in the mechanism known as a keroterion. In the same museum he learned of the practice of ostracism, the custom whereby Athenian citizens could be expelled from their city for a period of ten years. The practice was introduced by Kleisthenes in c. 508 BCE and was used within the subsequent twenty years.

If a sufficient number of citizens – perhaps six thousand – wrote the same name on pottery sherds, or ostraca, the ostracized person had to leave Athens within ten days. Several names on excavated ostraca are surprising because they are heroes and leaders known to us through other written sources: names like Pericles, Kimon, and Themistocles. This was done without bringing any specific charge against the man. The rationale, Menno imagined, was likely the same as the practice of shunning from his own heritage. Some members were viewed as threatening the stability, harmony, and wellbeing of the group, and were cast out. But of course, private motives played their part in choosing the candidate to be removed from the group. Regardless, the examples of shunning and ostracism were harsh measures put into practice for the supposed benefit of the collective.

Mykonos

Archaeological Museum of Mykonos

A former school colleague knew of Menno's predisposition toward the ethics of going to war and recommended that he pay a visit to the Archaeological Museum on the Island of Mykonos. The island was en route to his next planned stop in the Aegean islands. He departed the following day from Raphina, for the island best known for its pristine Cycladic architecture, nude beaches, and summer celebrities. Menno avoided the island's customary allurements and made his way to the museum. That it was open was his first reward.

Menno was in search of one piece in the museum's collection. The attendant directed him to a large urn, or pithos, 1.4 metres in height, almost that of an adult. It was a burial urn that had contained bones; it was discovered in a well on the island in the 1960s. Archaeologists dated the urn to the first half of the 7th century BCE. That is, the potter fashioned the urn and relief within a generation or two of the composition of Homer's *Iliad*.

The setting of the subject depicted on the urn's relief is the Trojan War, and the focus is a moment at the end of the war. The relief is noteworthy because in place of featuring the glory, heroism, and valour of battle, the subject is entirely different. The artist chose another vantage point to observe the ten-year conflict. The neck of the pithos depicts the descent of the Greeks from the wooden horse, and the panels below illustrate the warriors attacking women and children.

Of special interest to Menno were a number of scenes in relief depicting the struggle between a woman and man over a child. The woman is overcome in her efforts to shield the child. The scenes so vividly recalled the narrative in Book VI of the *Iliad*, not to mention the end of Euripides' play, the Trojan Women. Menno attributed names to the potter's figures – ones from the *Iliad*. In Homer's account of the capture of Troy, the poet draws attention to Andromache, widow of Hector who was slain by Achilles. Her young son, it has been decided by the Achaeans, is to be thrown to his death off the high walls of Troy. Andromache, mother of Astyanax, struggles to protect her child from Neoptolemos, son of Achilles. But the calm rationale of the Achaeans is that the child cannot be given the opportunity to avenge his father's death, were he to grow to manhood. And tragically, Neoptolemos has his way.

To Menno, it was indeed inexplicable that if the *Iliad* was a celebration of the heroic ideal where one proves oneself through valour in battle, one would then be drawn to a scene of the hero going about killing children. Perhaps the poet and the potter have created works of art with another agenda, one of questioning the way things are. For Menno and few others of his bias it was apparent that the madness inherent in violence and strife led exactly to this end—the sacrifice of the innocent, in this case a child. At the same time, Menno knew that the intent of the potter could never be demonstrated with certainty.

Paros

Paros Archaeological Museum

On a clear day on Mykonos, you can see the Island of Paros, to the southwest. It was Menno's next stop. In the past he had studied a selection of Greek lyric poetry from the archaic period. One of the earliest voices revealed to a modern reader was that of Archilochus. His work is preserved in quotations found in later works and fragments found on papyrus in Egypt. He is thought to have lived around 650 BCE, the son of Telesicles and a slave Enipo. It was often repeated that Archilochus was remembered in antiquity in the same breath as Homer and Hesiod. It was his composition, *The Hymn to Heracles*, that was sung at the Olympic games, at the crowning of each victor. He was given credit for his inventiveness in the use of the iambic metre, for he was both musician and poet, in addition to his profession as a mercenary. His poetry provides a unique opportunity to glimpse one of the earliest portraits in western literature. Because Archilochus was a mercenary, he made his living in service to Ares, in addition to Dionysus. Not surprisingly, a large number of existing fragments of his poetry deal with the experience of war.

When Menno arrived at Paroikia on the Island of Paros he asked directions to the cave of Archilochus. In Plutarch he had read the story of Koiranos. Koiranos of Paros, or possibly Miletos, came across fishermen who had captured dolphins in their nets near Byzantium. He proceeded to ransom the dolphins to save their lives. Some time thereafter a fifty-oared galley capsized in the strait between Naxos and Paros. Forty-nine aboard perished. Koiranos was on that galley but was saved by a dolphin that carried him ashore at the site facing the Island of Syros, known since then as Archilochus' cave. Years later when Koiranos died, his funeral pyre was along the shore, opposite which dolphins assembled and remained for the funeral, as a last farewell.

Such connectivity between humans and other beings interested Menno. As well the connectivity between different eras, words that survived from antiquity: on Paros the word 'ράχη' (which meant the back of a donkey) was still in use. In antiquity, the term was also used to mean a mountain ridge, or 'ράχισ'. Yet, it was the rare vantage point found in Archilochus' poetry that drew Menno to Paros.

On his way to Kakapetra Menno meandered through the charming narrow walkways of Paroikia. On one of the main market streets he spotted a familiar figure. Was it? Yes it was Virgil! He was on his way to Chania on the Island of Crete, hoping to connect with Greeks and MCC staff still working near Chania. Menno thought it was quite the coincidence that he would again meet the hiker from Pharsala. Not giving it much more thought, Menno invited Virgil to join him on his walk.

It took Menno and Virgil less than an hour to walk from the town to Kakapetra, just south and west of the harbour. There Menno did more than read his notes; he more or less made a presentation, before a predictable critic, explaining the following:

According to a third century BCE inscription by Mnesiepes found at the poet's cult site on Paros, this was the place to be chosen where Archilochus began his illustrious life as poet and musician, here just outside Paroikia. Archilochus, a young lad, was sent by his father to fetch a heifer from the meadow, to be sold at the market. At dawn, the lad was leading the heifer through the slippery rocks of Kakapetra when he encountered a number of young women. After a brief exchange they enquired if the heifer was for sale, adding that they were willing to pay a worthy sum for the animal. Upon acceptance of the offer the women and heifer promptly disappeared, leaving a lyre in their place. Young Archilochus immediately intuited who the women really were; he understood that he had been approached and chosen by the Muses.

While sitting on one of the granite boulders of Kakapetra, Menno withdrew from his backpack a small publication of fragments of Archilochus' poetry. Without the benefit of many complete poems enough remained of images and portraits and experiences to suggest first-hand observations by the poet.[1] War was not pretty:

'where oh where Exias is the luckless host mustering?' and
' the foe is favoured with woesome guest gifts'
And of the bodies left to decompose:
'with such a man the field is fattened'.

Archilochus had no desire to rule over others, nor was he tempted by monetary reward (by the gold of Gyges). When the son of Peisistratos set sail for Thasos and treasure he fashioned misfortune for his fellows: 'for private gain they sacrificed the common good.'

In another fragment, Archilochus confesses that he 'left behind his shield, beside some bush; now some Thracian is enjoying the use of it; what is important I saved myself—you can always get another one'. Another similar sentiment appears later,

'No man gets honour or glory of his countrymen once he is dead'.

It was said that Archilochus was driven out of Sparta for his unheroic stance, one in contrast to their own poet Tyrtaeus. His famous exhortation was that you come home carrying your shield, or fall upon it when killed in battle. Neither does Archilochus fall in line with expectations when it came to respect for superiors:

> 'I love not a tall general...
> nor one proud of his hair.'

If there remained any question about the honour gained in war:

> 'of seven that lie dead
> whom we overtook in the pursuit
> we are the thousand slayers'.

It seemed to Menno that Archilochus' poetry upset the rationale for going to war and in doing so rattled the very foundation of recruitment in the reasons given to enter the fray. When it came to the outcome of battle there was much to fear, much that was woesome. He challenged the violent quest for profit because it brought grief for one's fellows and for the common interest. Beyond that, the honour and glory that Achilles and Hector strove for do you no good when you are dead. We strive instead to live — which is a most troubling message to propagate in times of war and recruitment. Nor does revenge, or paying back the one committing wrong solve anything:

> 'I sinned and I think this retribution has overtaken another.'

Menno recalled that αμαρτάνω meant to miss the mark, as in archery competition. It meant to fail of one's purpose, or to err. The root is shared in the New Testament where αμαρτία is translated as sin.

When he had finished, Virgil – with that smile in his eyes – asked if Menno really thought Archilochus was a pacifist. He did not wait for a response. Virgil was convinced that confession was needed to precede our attempts to live a more godly life. And he conceded that based on what Menno had quoted, it seemed that this fellow, the poet, saw with clear eyes what warfare and conflict were all about. Yet, this civilization was not known for its peacemakers, and the poet was a mercenary after all.

Virgil asked further: 'Are you not remaking the ancient Greeks, from a few slivers of evidence, into a narrative that you imagine? Maybe you are inventing some kind of paradise, one that exists elsewhere, but not here. Think on it.' Menno did think on it and became rather glum. They walked without conversation back to Paroikia where they had a coffee together. Then Virgil left to meet the Minos Line ferry to Crete.

Before leaving Paros, Menno entered the Eastern Orthodox Church of the Holy Virgin whose dormition is celebrated on August 15. It is thought to be one of the oldest churches in all of Greece. Tradition has it that St Helena, mother of Constantine the Great, stopped at Paros in the fourth century en route to the Holy Land. A vow to build a church there is illustrated in the very early baptistry, dedicated to John the Baptist, to the west of the present church. Some say that under Emperor Justinian a church was begun on the site in the sixth century CE, when he appointed Isidore, an architect of Saint Sophia in Constantinople, to oversee completion of the work. In this church, Menno came across an icon of Saint Theoktiste, a young nun abducted from Methymna on Lesbos, who escaped on Paros and died on this island. Menno was determined to read more about her when time allowed.

A small icon museum, holding a rare collection of art from various island churches and monasteries, was to the right of the courtyard. One icon drew Menno's eye. It was a 17th century icon of the Nativity and the adoration of the magi. The icon depicted a shift of the world's centre. Joseph sits in the foreground, grappling with what the arrival of this child means. Surrounding the Christ child in the manger are shepherds, sheep, and donkeys who gaze at the child from the right, and above are angels looking on in approval. The heavens themselves have relocated the star above the stable in Bethlehem, and the magi (a priestly caste of wisemen) arrive bearing gifts. The artist has painted several levels and spheres of recognition and adoration, and has included – interestingly – the priestly caste and possibly the wisdom of the East!

The accumulated wisdom of the East – of older civilizations – is present in this icon, in a long tradition predating the artist's work by more than two thousand years. Since learning of the seven sages of ancient Greece Menno longed to know what exactly constituted wisdom in this era. And more particularly, what were the teachings of these sages? He had noted that four out of the seven sages came from the western shores of Asia Minor, the land of ancient trade routes from the East. It seems likely that they had been exposed to the enquiries and discoveries of different cultures along the routes, so that more than mere merchandise was exchanged.

Lindos, Rhodes

Lindos Acropolis

In pursuit of the sages and their wisdom, Menno boarded a ferry at Paros bound for Rhodes. The journey was a milk-run – one taking a full day, with stops at small Aegean and Dodecanese islands along the route. Shortly before arriving at Rhodes, Menno grabbed a sandwich in the ship's cafeteria. Seated near him was a group, he later learned, from Berea, Kentucky. He could overhear their conversation and learned that they were Quakers en route to Lindos to visit St Paul's Chapel. (In Acts it was written that St Paul stopped at Rhodes after leaving Kos.)

Menno enjoyed meeting fellow travellers. When he informed them that he too was going to Lindos they assumed it was for the same reason that had brought them to Rhodes.

He explained that his mission was different; he was visiting because it was home to an ancient Greek sage. The Quakers were curious about the sage's identity and teachings. As their boat entered the harbour and the passengers were preparing to disembark, Menno offered to meet them in Lindos where he would tell them about the sage Kleoboulos.

At Rhodes Menno left behind Mussolini's architectural contribution to the main town, and the city of the Knights of Saint John, and made his way by bicycle to Lindos, on the southwest shore of the island. Along the way, just outside the town of Rhodes, Menno observed a priest sacrificing a rooster. The rooster had just been decapitated and its blood was being shed into the freshly poured cement foundation for a new house. The house would be blessed through this ritual.

It was much later in the day that Menno arrived in Lindos, and as it was a small village he readily encountered the group of Quakers. At the site of the ancient acropolis, with the stunning relief of a trireme behind him, Menno briefly explained that Lindos was the home of Kleoboulos, a monarch of the city (according to Plutarch). He inaugurated the building program on Lindos' acropolis, including the Temple of Athena Lindia. Not surprisingly, Kleoboulos also studied in Egypt. He was acknowledged as one of the seven sages, and today we have a minor planet or asteroid named after him.

The teachings of this sage proved of great interest to Menno.[2] There was the maxim that saying too much whilst knowing too little characterized most people. It was better always to listen, rather than talk, and to be fond of learning. Virtue should be sought over seeking pleasure. And injustice should be avoided.

Beyond these exhortations there were several that delivered Menno back to the roots of his own upbringing. People were not supposed to do anything by force. Persuasion was the better course, and people were expected to ready themselves for reconciliation after conflict. The word 'symbiosis' helped Menno remember the Greek term for 'to reconcile:' Συμβιβάζω meant to bring together, to bring to terms, or to reconcile. We ought to do good to a friend, but also to our enemy, and to make of him a friend and educate our children to put an end to enmity. Altogether, Menno's roots reminded him of well-rounded counsel to put an end to strife and mitigate its effects.

After the review of the sparse threads of Kleoboulos' teachings Menno awaited the Quakers' response with great interest, not the least because they were part of one of the few peace churches. Menno waited, and after a few moments passed he asked what they thought about this sage. Menno had to remind himself that Friends worship together in silence allowing their hearts and minds to open to the presence of God. Thus a lengthy silence persisted, until a member of the Society spoke. He announced that he would quote George Fox: "I saw into that which was without end, things which cannot be uttered, and of the greatness and infinitude of the love of God, which cannot be expressed by words." The group and Menno had been standing in a circle, until each of the Quakers approached Menno to shake his hand. It was unclear to Menno what was going on, but perhaps no more needed saying. Or, so he hoped.

Menno remained in Lindos for a few days and surveyed the castle, the acropolis and surrounding countryside. His thoughts returned to Kleoboulos, especially given how remarkable his teachings were, considering their apparent coincidence with the doctrine of non-resistance held by the 16th century Anabaptists and Quakers.

Tristomo, Karpathos

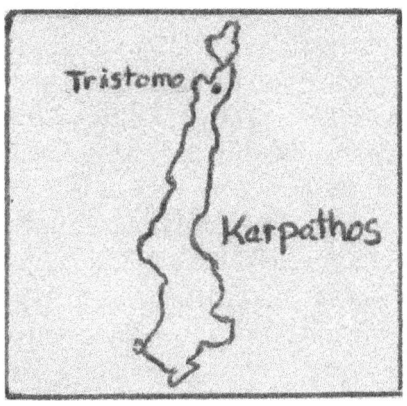

Tristomo, Karpathos

Menno altered his plans while on Rhodes; he had first intended to stop next at the home of another sage. Instead he decided to take a ferry to Karpathos, an island between Rhodes and Crete, most easily reached from the former. Menno had read about a Dorian decree from the third century BCE that was kept in the British Museum. The inscription on the decree was made in marble and was found at Tristomo, on Karpathos. For posterity, it recorded the contribution of a doctor over a lifetime of selfless dedication to others in need.[3] The dedication revealed the following:

'Menokritos, a doctor, practiced in Vrykus for twenty years asking for no recompense for his services, not even a drachma, whilst he himself lived in poverty. He energetically addressed the needs of the sick, including total strangers not known to him. Throughout his years of service, he did not avoid the paths to the most remote habitations to lend assistance and look after the sick, all without charging any fee. In return for this service to humankind the citizens of Vrykus wish to honour Menokritos with the gift of a golden crown. So that his fame is proclaimed far and wide. And a plaque is to be erected, featuring his service, in the Poseidon Porthmius Temple.'

When Menno paid his visit to Tristomo it was home to only a handful of inhabitants. It hosted a well-protected tiny harbour and was surrounded by inhospitable terrain. Notwithstanding, there was an abundance of donkey trails, mostly used for hiking in more recent times. The views across the north shore of Karpathos were stunning and comprised the main reward for hikers, along with the peaceful quiet for contemplating the place of medicine in antiquity.

The tradition of healing without recompense would continue, remarkably, for centuries. Northeast of Karpathos on the Asia Minor coast was once the Hittite region of Cilicia (in the South of modern Turkey). Cilicia was a part of the Roman Province of Syria. Here, during the persecution of Emperor Diocletian two Christian doctors – Kosmas and Damian – were arrested by order of the prefect of Cilicia, and under torture they were commanded to recant their faith. According to church tradition, they were crucified, stoned, and then beheaded.

A painting of the martyrdom by Fra Angelico can be viewed in the Louvre, with haloes lingering over their severed heads. Three younger brothers were thought to have lost their lives at the same time, c. 287 CE, at the seaport of Aegea. It is alleged that they were all killed while being faithful to their calling. Their lives were lived in keeping with the injunction found in Matthew 10:8, 'Freely have you received, freely give.' Kosmas and Damian refused monetary reward for their practice of medicine. As a consequence, the saints have been venerated to this day as Ἅγιοι Ανάργυροι, the penniless or 'silverless' saints who refused recompense for their services.

On an earlier trip, Menno had visited the Monastery of Kosmas and Damian on Paros where, from a great height on the mountain, it looked down on Paroikia. At the time he marvelled at the continuation of the tradition of benevolence of physicians, from its pagan origins through centuries of service into the Christian era and beyond. Menno carried these thoughts with him as he left the main port of Karpathos to return to Rhodes. From there he took a ferry for a short sailing North to the Island of Kos and its harbour of welcoming palm trees.

Kos

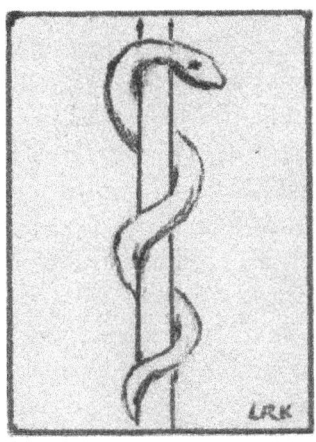

Rod of Asclepios

It was on this leg of the trip that Menno met a finely dressed middle-aged woman who sat down in an adjacent seat on the upper deck bench where he was reading. She enquired whether Menno had been to Kos before and mentioned that she was a doctor from Munich and had visited Kos more than once. In their conversation, Menno learned that the doctor had an interest in early Greek medicine and the relationship of its practice to contemporary schools of philosophy. In the time that it took to sail to Kos, the two decided to explore the site together, and Menno asked if the doctor might lead the way. She recounted much that Menno had learned in his studies.

The doctor reminded Menno that it was here at Kos that the practice of medicine in the classical period was advanced. Once again, the Greeks inherited waves of influence in this field from older civilizations – from Egypt, Minoan Crete, the Phoenicians, Assyro-Babylonians, and Mesopotamia. It was here that Hippocrates was born (460-377 BCE), and where a thriving medical training centre evolved. It was coloured by earlier Greek philosophical thought that emphasized ethical behaviour and the principle of harmony. Hippocrates' writings revealed a rational approach to the study of medicine, one that focused on prognosis and treatment. The approach was based on logical reasoning, observation, and the healing powers of nature. It endeavoured to embrace the whole human being, including its physical, mental, and spiritual aspects. Many of Hippocrates' writings were collected by the third century BCE and left with the library in Alexandria.

Menno had brought with him a translation of the Oath of Hippocrates, the one of old that formed a basis for our modern use.[4] He found it of benefit to read it once again:

'I swear by Apollo the physician and Asklepios, and Hygeia and Panacea, and all the gods and goddesses, that, according to my ability and judgment, I will keep this Oath and this stipulation to reckon him who taught me this Art equally dear to me as my parents, to share my substance with him, and relieve his necessities if required; to look upon his offspring in the same footing as my own brothers, and to teach them this Art, if they shall wish to learn it, without fee or stipulation; and that by precept, lecture, and every other mode of instruction, I will impart a knowledge of the Art to my own sons, and those of my teachers, and to disciples bound by a stipulation and oath according to the law of medicine, but to none others. I will follow that system of regimen which, according to my ability and judgment, I consider for the benefit of my patients, and abstain from whatever is deleterious and mischievous. I will give no deadly medicine to anyone if asked, nor support any such counsel; and in like manner I will not give to a woman a pessary to produce abortion. With purity and holiness I will pass my life and practice my Art. I will not cut persons labouring under the stone, but will leave this to be done by men who are practitioners of this work. Into whatever house I enter, I will go into them for the benefit of the sick, and will abstain from every voluntary act of mischief and corruption; and, further, from the seduction of females and males, of freemen and slaves. Whatever, in connection with my professional service, or not in connection with it, I see or hear, in the life of men, which ought not to be spoken of abroad, I will not divulge, as reckoning that all such should be kept secret. While I continue to keep this Oath unviolated, may it be granted to me to enjoy life and the practice of the Art, respected by all men, in all times. But should I trespass and violate this Oath, may the reverse be my lot.'

The doctor wished to add her personal views to their conversation, which Menno welcomed. There was that which scholars agreed upon. From Hippocrates' time medical diagnosis and treatment were placed on a scientific base, emphasizing the observation of patients and their response to applied remedies. Secondly, there was considerable agreement that Pythagoras enters the story here. His emphasis on harmony was important; that is, the body's health has much to do with the working together of the body's parts, and the balance of exercise and diet and mental composure were underlined in treatments here at Kos. Unfortunately there was much less agreement on the matters of healing, the role of the spirit, and the nature of the gods. The doctor left Menno with the thought that there was much yet to learn about the connection between the spirit and healing.

Menno felt that the profession was indeed one of mercy, as evidenced in the Oath. It was also one of egalitarian purpose, where male and female, freeman and slave were of one status. Menno had much to ponder as he made his way to have his dinner, not the least the fortuitous meeting with the doctor and the introduction to her interests.

While enjoying a carafe of retsina in a fish taverna he temporarily left behind his customary taciturn nature. As the taverna was small he could engage in conversation with Greeks at neighbouring tables. One of whom was Manolis, a local fisherman. It was here that Menno informed Manolis that he was trying to find a way to cross the strait to Bodrum in Turkey.

Bodrum-Halicarnassus

Herodotus

In antiquity, the place was called Halicarnassus, the birthplace of the classical historian Herodotus. The fisherman volunteered that he had a καράβι – something like a sloop, big enough for two passengers and a few fish, and he thought he could oblige and bring Menno to Bodrum. As he stroked his chin, Manolis thought they could set out soon, if the winds cooperated, and if he might enjoy another carafe of retsina. And so, the men came to a jolly agreement.

Upon arrival the next day, the first impression of Bodrum was made by the imposing Bodrum Castle, built by the Knights Hospitaller in the fifteenth century. Menno had read that one of the seven wonders of the world was to be found here: the mausoleum from c. 350 BCE, a monument and tomb of Mausolus, ruler of Caria. It had been adorned by a number of sculptures made by leading Greek artists, including the sculpture of Skopas of Paros. After one too many earthquakes, and the 're-dedication' of architectural members, scattered blocks of stone and levelled column drums were all that remained for Menno to see.

Notwithstanding the allure of mausoleums and castles, the wonder that Menno came to remember was the person Herodotus of Halicarnassus. Menno chose to meditate upon his subject in the remarkable second century BCE Greco-Roman theatre, with a seating capacity of about four thousand. On that day, Menno was the sole theatre goer, as the few tourists in the theatre had vanished over the lunch hour.

In the second book of his *Histories*, Herodotus draws comparisons between Greek and Egyptian deities, often identifying one god with their counterpart in the other land. Herodotus seeks equivalencies and finds them. For the historian, Zeus is not like Amun, rather, he is Amun. A myth recounted at Thebes in Egypt, likely by Egyptian priests, relates how Zeus hid his identity from Heracles, by holding a ram's head before him and covering himself with its fleece. Either Zeus was dressing up like Amun, or was suggesting to the Egyptians that they were the same.

Similarly, the Egyptian goddess Isis came to be revered in Greece as Io. Herodotus , while not certain, may be pointing to the universality of the gods; that is the same gods, but by different names. At the same time, Herodotus would have learned that knowledge of some of the Greek gods came from Egypt, which was a much older civilization.

In another case, Herodotus identifies Dionysus in the Egyptian god Osiris, for both reign over fertility and both are dismembered and resurrected. Other comparisons underline not only Herodotus' habit of thought, but his commonalities with his fellow Greeks. Greek thought often sought unity and order, and was given to seeing things as a whole. It seemed essential to Greek sanity. In keeping with this principle, the number of gods was reduced over time, and natural laws governing the universe and moral precepts were perceived as the same. Ananke and Moira (Necessity and Fate) were expressions of Zeus' will. The world of gods and men was seen as one, where the gods in both Greece and Egypt represent immanent laws and conditions of human existence. The particular and the universal aspects of the same action are joined (as in the relationship of microcosm and macrocosm). To Greek minds, particularly in the archaic period, a law or universal principle was the same as an act of the gods. Or, in other words, the gods prefigure collectively a world order, the dictates of natural philosophy, and the framework of life. Altogether, for the ancient Greeks, this was how the world worked and how it could be understood.

This way of understanding human existence in relation to the world we find ourselves in, and in relation to God, or the gods, was not altogether strange for Menno. He had wondered about the shades of meaning of Logos, Λόγος, in the Gospel of John. For Philo, a contemporary of Jesus, Logos was divine reason, that which penetrated the material world and comprised all the ideas of the finite in the world. Logos was too the mediating principle between God and matter, which was in existence from the beginning (cf Pythagoras' similar point in the example of 1/3 and 3/9 where the number three is the mediating principle between 1 and 9).

As the spoken word issues from thought, the Logos of God creates the world and forms the outward communication of God with human beings. Logos here embraces all the workings and revelations of God in the world, the ideas and forces that fashion the very framework of our world. For John, that important mediator between God and the world was Jesus, or the Logos. He was related to God as the word to the idea, and was present with God from the beginning.

As Menno sat in the ancient theatre in Bodrum, he felt at one with Herodotus' search for equivalencies between Greek and Egyptian gods, thereby reducing the multiplicity of gods to an overarching unity. He also felt that there was a discernible thread connecting earlier ancient Greek thought and that of Philo and John. Menno then imagined two circles that partly overlapped where there could be found synchronicity between the thought of antiquity and his own framework of understanding which he had inherited from the sixteenth century.

Miletos

Thales

Menno soon had to bid Herodotus adieu, as his fisherman Manolis had found another ψαράς who would deliver him to the Ionian shore opposite the ancient city of Priene. Menno's new captain would not disclose why he could not stop at Miletos. As he sailed by the delta of the Maeander River Menno recalled that much of the little body of knowledge about Thales had Aristotle as its source. It was Aristotle who also reminded his readers that the names of the seven sages first appeared in the Protagoras dialogue of Plato. Thales, one of the seven, is credited by Aristotle with being the founder of natural philosophy.[5]

Thales famously posited that water was the primary principle of the cosmos, and he also theorized about the causes of earthquakes, proclaimed that the earth was a sphere, and described the nature of solar eclipses. He is credited with predicting the eclipse of 585 BCE, when the Medians and Lydians – in the midst of battle – sensed an awful power, ceased fighting, and reached a peace agreement.

What interested Menno was Thales' view that the soul was the cause of movement and that it pervaded and enlivened the whole universe. In abbreviated form, 'everything is full of the gods.' If Menno understood correctly, Thales' belief was not that different from that of the Greek Orthodox Church; namely, that there is a connection between every atom in the universe and the Mind of God.

The names of the seven sages were proposed early in the sixth century BCE, and at some point the sages gathered at Delphi, where they offered their maxims to Apollo. The most memorable two were 'γνῶθι σαυτόν,' know yourself, and 'μέτρων ἀριστον,' nothing in excess. After Thales' home receded from Menno's view, he recalled the astounding number of colonies Miletos founded on the shores of the Black Sea, some of them in Crimea and adjacent shores in the Ukraine, indeed where much later many of Menno's family and cousins hailed from. This coincidence and the later proselytism of Russians by Greeks possibly offered an explanation for the presence of a handful of Greek words that entered his forbears' vocabulary: watermelon or 'arbusen from καρπύζι', coat or 'paltau from παλτό', easter (bread) 'paska from Πάσχα', 'chalva from χαλβᾶσ', mosquitoes or 'midje from μύγα' and so on. While Menno did not find such discoveries to be overly significant on their own, he nevertheless found the journey of ideas and remnants of words fascinating. So too with the stories from Russia that Menno was told when he was young, and the images of this world – some given birth by the exquisite folk painting of artist and farmer, Henry Pauls, whom he had met when he was only a child.

Priene

Bouleterion of Priene

Priene, originally a Carian city according to Pausanias, was likely settled by Ionians in the eighth century BCE. It was home to Bias, one of the sages mentioned in the Protagoras of Plato – the reason for Menno's next chosen destination.[6] During Bias' lifetime, the city came under the rule of the Lydians, and in turn under the Persians, in 546 BCE. Priene over time became an important centre of cultural exchange between the East and Greece. The city was also home to the Panionian sanctuary, the federation of twelve Greek cities, and Samos, which formed a bastion of freedom from foreign (Persian) rule, thereby making it a cultural and spiritual centre.

Upon landing, Menno chose to roam about the ancient city, which had just become a UNESCO heritage site. What he saw was not the city of Bias, but a later one, the relocated Priene on the slope of the Mycale Mountain ridge. This city dated from the later Hellenistic period. On his walk Menno discovered the defensive walls, paved streets complete with drains, a grid of clay water pipes, the lined columns, or stoas of the marketplace, and the five remaining columns of the Temple of Athena. In addition he noted a place of worship 'for the Egyptian gods,' a largely preserved theatre, and the best preserved parliamentary chamber in antiquity: the bouleterion, or council chambers of Priene.

It was in the bouleterion that Menno chose to sit and have his lunch. There he tried to retrieve the life and teachings of Bias. Altogether, the seven sages seem to have despaired of strife and violence, and this during the pinnacle of the heroic age! In part what is now known of Bias comes from the second century CE. A good deal is found in the writings of Diogenes Laertius, in his book *The Lives and Opinions of Eminent Philosophers*.

In Diogenes Laertius we learn of Bias' exhortation to accept things, having procured them by persuasion, not by force. When presented with a tripod inscribed with the words, 'for the wise,' he refused to receive it because he believed it belonged not to him but to Apollo. At the same time, he advocated cherishing wisdom on the journey to old age because it was more lasting than any possession. He acknowledged that to bear change for the worse with grace was most difficult. He further taught that it was a disease of the mind to have no regard for the misfortune of others.

Menno remembered reading somewhere that Bias paid a ransom for a number of sisters taken as prisoners of war. He educated them as if they were his own daughters and then sent them home to their father in Messina. As a judge, Bias gained renown for his fair rulings in disputes for what was right. In keeping with his reputation, he counselled against praising an undeserving man only for his riches.

As Menno sat in the bouleterion, the sun's rays were filtered through high clouds, bathing the site in a soft light. It made Menno smile to imagine Bias basking in the same light twenty-five centuries ago. What a proposition, to suggest we are unwell of mind when we go our own way and disregard others' misfortunes! Like the day's light, for Menno there was much that was merciful and kindly in Bias' life.

After reflecting, Menno returned to the harbour of Priene to find a conveyance northward, and by sea, if possible. There were sailboats with tourists in the harbour.

Lesbos, Mytilene, and Eressos

Fortress at Mytilene

One crew agreed to take him on as far as the Island of Samos. There he would take a ferry on to Chios and Lesbos. Two days later Menno arrived at Mytilene on the Island of Lesbos where he made his way to the ancient acropolis – a walk of less than an hour from the harbour. The remnants from antiquity had largely vanished, leaving structures from the sixth century CE, possibly built during the reign of Justinian, in turn to be replaced by the more recent castle of Mytilene. Here Menno found a bench to rest and journey back to the time of Pittakos.[7]

Pittakos (640-568 BCE) was a general who was victorious over the Athenians who came to lay siege to Lesbos. In place of engaging forces on both sides, Pittakos proposed that two men engage in combat, one from each side. The outcome would determine the winning side, and at the same time prevent bloodshed for their soldiers on both sides. The proposal was accepted by the Athenians. With his broad sword Pittakos defeated Phrynon, the Athenian chosen to fight him. Tradition has it that the Athenians withdrew and, in gratitude to Pittakos, the demos of Mytilene supported him and made him lawgiver for ten years.

Pittakos, one of the seven 'σόφοι', or sages, proffered much of the same practical advice as the other sages: it is a hard thing to be a really good man, to know what opportunities to choose, and whatever you do, to do it well. Power shows the man. Menno recalled the story told of the murder of Pittakos' son, Tyrrhaeus. His father's response was entirely out of character with the time, when revenge would naturally follow. Instead, Pittakos dismissed the murderer, allegedly proclaiming that 'pardon is better than punishment,' and 'mercy is better than vengeance.' Menno found that the ancient Greek term for 'pardon,' συγχωρέω, connotes coming together, or giving way. Ελεήμων was a familiar term from the Latin Mass, often translated as 'merciful.'

In keeping with his reputation, but also with his fellow sages he counselled: 'do not reproach a man with his misfortunes, fearing that Nemesis may overtake you.' And in the same spirit: 'forbear to speak evil not only of your friends, but also of your enemies.'

Menno felt it was important to remember that in Greek the term δύναμις denoted strength, force, or might. The same attribute was used in reference to the spoken word, which mattered greatly. Moreover, the foundation of his teachings was very similar to the golden rule: 'do not to your neighbour what you would take ill from him.' While this expression is a negative version of 'do good to your neighbour,' it is yet one of the earliest exhortations of such clarity.

Pittakos died in the third year of the 52nd Olimpiad, or 568 BCE, by our reckoning. Diogenes Laertius leaves his readers with the epitaph of Pittakos:

'Here holy Lesbos, with a mother's woe
Bewails her Pittakos, whom death laid low.'
(trans. Robert Hicks)

Before bidding Lesbos adieu, Menno took a bus across the island to its west shore. Along the way he was greeted by a severe landscape of rock sculptures and boulders, and a noteworthy petrified forest. In the spring, the rocky terrain would be decorated with wildflowers, giving inspiration to one Theophrastus, who was born here and would later be considered the father of botany.

Along the way, Menno asked the driver if the bus stopped at Methymna. It did not, he was informed. He was overheard by a company of women sitting in the front seats of the bus. They were young and attractive and while they showed little interest in Menno, they asked what was in Methymna, as though not wishing to miss anything.

Menno obliged and related the story of Saint Theoktiste, who was born in Methymna. She was orphaned at a young age and was placed in a nunnery. While there, the nunnery was raided and she was abducted by the Saracens to be sold into slavery. In crossing the Aegean Sea a storm forced them to take shelter at Paros. There she luckily escaped and spent her remaining days. Because Paros' population had been decimated by similar raids, there were few people to be found on the island when Theoktiste escaped. There she lived a pious and ascetic life, surviving, it is alleged, on figs and lupin seeds and little else. After some time had passed, a hunter visited Paros where he discovered the ascetic who asked that she be brought communion. This he did on a later trip, but found she had died. He thought she must be a saint and therefore removed a finger as a holy relic to take with him. However, he could not leave due to uncooperative winds. He returned the finger and all was well, and after a time Paros claimed her as a Parian saint.

After the brief telling of the story, the leader of the group, Anastasia – whose name in Greek meant awakening or resurrection – approached Menno and offered to return the favour at Skala Eressos, if that was where he was going. She felt it necessary to explain that while she was the leader of this group of women, she was not Lesbian herself. She was Greek, but her company of women hailed from various European countries.

Menno's destination was indeed Skala Eressos where the poetess Sappho was born. Menno's former professor, H. D. F. Kitto, had once announced that learning ancient Greek would be worth the effort, if nothing but Sappho had remained in the language, and the fragments of Sappho are fragmentary indeed. Kitto was in good company in his love for the words of Sappho. It is said that upon hearing one of Sappho's lyrics, Solon the poet and lawgiver requested that it be sung again, 'so he might take it to heart and die.' For good reason, centuries later, Plato would refer to Sappho as the tenth muse.

When Anastasia and Menno met at Skala Eressos, she spent an hour or more reading from the fragments of Sappho, and adding comments. She told Menno that nine volumes of Sappho's poetry were lost when fire destroyed the library in Alexandria. What would remain until our day was acknowledgment that Lesbos, particularly Eressos, was the etymological springboard for women who love women. Indeed, it was Sappho's vocation to instruct young girls. It is entirely unclear what her instruction entailed. Was it a kind of academy for girls, a finishing school of sorts? Was her circle comprised of mistresses, hetairai, who were taught to compose lyric verses? Perhaps her circle of girls – her 'Θίασος – was a gathering of young women dedicated to love, beauty, and mutual life. Anastasia thought the dedication to love and mutuality comprised an enviable vocation. The English word amoeba, signifying the capacity for interchanging, helped Menno recall the Greek word αμοίβη, denoting atonement or mutuality. Menno preferred this understanding of the poet's vocation as well, and wished that more of her writings had survived.

Anastasia and Menno agreed to meet later for dinner. That evening their comfort with one another resulted in animated conversation on subjects that they each found interesting. Anastasia was surprised that Menno would know of a less well-known saint, like Theoktiste. The saint was another example, she thought, of the plight of women in a violent world. Menno explained that he had visited Paros where he learned of her in the pilgrimage church in Paroikia. Before they parted ways, Anastasia expressed an interest in whether their paths would cross again. Menno shared his travel plans and his wish that they would see each other again. She suggested that she might be on the Island of Kimilos, near Milos, after a few weeks. And so Anastasia left to be with her group and Menno to find a room. That night he dreamed of a female figure, one barely discernible. Yet he could make out that she was partly a poetess, partly a saint, and partly a new friend.

Chios

Daskalopetra, Chios

Back at Mytilene, Menno boarded a ferry of the Dodecanese Line, bound for Chios. A number of places claimed the birth-place of Homer, and the two most serious contenders were Chios and Smyrna (opposite on the mainland of Asia Minor). Upon arrival at Chios, Menno made his way to the Archaeological Museum, where he studied the cosmopolitan nature of Chios in the early archaic period.

The collection included many things: faience objects, earthenware decorated with opaque coloured glazes which were imported from Naukratis (the Greek trading post in Egypt), Lotus blossoms inscribed in marble from an entablature, early amphorae for transporting salted fish, oil, wine, cereals and cheese for Canaan; and some vases from the time of Sappho.

As he left the museum, who was coming toward the entrance but Virgil! Menno was normally a bit slow to draw conclusions, but this coincidental meeting made Menno begin to wonder how this could be happening. Was this the third crossing of paths? No time to ponder as Virgil was again his friendly talkative self. He was on his way to the port that served Mount Athos, home to over twenty monasteries and countless small settlements for ascetics and disciples. He decided to join Menno for a few days, as his schedule was quite open. So, Menno's second stop had to wait until the following morning.

Oral tradition held that Homer had taught on the Island of Chios. Menno found the alleged site, a short walk from the museum and known to all local islanders, near Vrondatos. Here was the 'school' site of scattered rock, known as 'δασκαλόπετρα,' or the teaching rock. At the rock, Menno introduced Virgil to Homer for the second time.

He began by telling Virgil that Homer's personal life evades certainties. The Hymn to Apollo of Delos refers to 'the blind man who dwells in rugged Chios.' Pindar, the archaic poet from Boeotia, and others, placed Homer in both Smyrna and Chios. Herodotus believed Homer to have lived no more than four hundred years before his time, the fifth century BCE. That is, Herodotus was approximately in agreement with scholarly estimates of our day, placing the poet in the eighth century BCE. It seems likely that Homer was a native of the western coast of Asia Minor or Ionia, as his poems are largely in the Ionic dialect.

He also shared with Virgil that before departing on his pilgrimage to Greece he had received a gift from a former professor, J. Winfield Fretz – a slim volume that should accompany him in his adventures. The professor had known of Menno's fondness for the epic poem of Homer, the *Iliad*. The publication given him was *The Iliad, or The Poem of Force*, by Simone Weil (a scholar who was at once philosopher, Greek literature professor, labourer, social worker, writer, resistance participant, and who wrote her analysis at age thirty-one, after the fall of France, and only three years before her untimely death). Here, seated on an outcrop of limestone, at 'δασκαλόπετρα' Menno settled into Simone Weil's exegesis of Western Civilization's earliest literary masterpiece.[8] And Virgil appeared quite interested as Menno described her interpretation.

Simone Weil sees the true subject of the Iliad as force – force which blinds the human spirit, makes a thing of a person, a thing being dragged behind a chariot, or made into a banquet for vultures and dogs, as the horses left behind long for their noble masters, as the horses rattle the empty chariots through the dust and gore of battle.

And destiny, in its blindness, automatically renders a just ruling: punishment in kind, as in the formulation 'he that takes the sword will perish by the sword.' Long before the observation is expressed in the Gospels we find it in Homer's epic: 'Ares is just, and kills those who kill.' No armour or shield, not even those made by the god Hephaistos, can stand in the way of retribution, the laws that re-establish balance after the abuse of power. Nemesis, in Greek thought, was at the beginning of their understanding of human nature and the cosmos. Concepts of limit and measure, as in 'μέτρων αριστον,' and equilibrium served with geometrical precision and rigour in the Greeks' pursuit of virtue.

In her interpretation of the *Iliad*, Weil points out there is a scattering of passages that remind Homer's audience of the soul that has room only for courage and love, those passages that shine light on the varied faces of love. This is the love that dispels the blindness of battle; namely, the tradition of hospitality that endures for generations. The love of father and mother for their son, of the son's love for parents, and brotherly love: in the case of Briseis, ' my three brothers whom the same mother bore me'. And the same was in evidence for conjugal love, 'better for me, losing you, to go under the earth.'

According to Weil, a beautiful form of love is the love of friendship between fellows in combat, if only to recover the body of the slain for proper funeral observances. The purest form of love is the friendship that overwhelms the hearts of mortal enemies – 'the crowning grace of war' in Weil's words. For Weil, what is absolutely unique in the *Iliad* is that next to the seemingly endless depiction of violent deeds is found a bitterness that issues from tenderness which embraces the entire human race, 'impartial as sunlight'. The *Iliad* is a poem wherein justice and love bathe the proceedings without a discursive slant, wherein the fortunes of all are laid bare without dissimulation, wherein both sides – the victors and the vanquished – are portrayed with equal clarity and nearness. It is an extraordinary sense of equity which breathes through the *Iliad*. It is not a story of one city against another, one way of life in contrast with another, but rather, it is the story of humanity.

In the end Weil saw what few see as clearly, and that which was dear to Menno: a thread, at least, of a continuum between the Iliad and the Gospels. This continuum is born by the effects that attend violence and force, in which none are spared, neither those who use it, nor those who suffer it. The continuum is where 'the shame of the coerced spirit is neither disguised, nor enveloped in facile pity, nor held up to scorn, where more than one spirit bruised and degraded by misfortune is offered for our admiration...' The same sense of human misery gives the Gospels that accent – one that is the mark of Greek genius. The accent in the Gospels on human misery as a precondition of justice and love is central to Weil's understanding. We cannot regard as fellow creatures, nor love others who have been separated from us by necessity and misfortune, to which all humans are subject at different times, without this precondition. She concludes, 'only he who has measured the dominion of force, and knows how not to respect it, is capable of love and justice.'

Menno had previously underlined passages of the Iliad, that Weil's work did not focus on, yet which were in agreement with her analysis. In Book VI an exquisite scene of 'inherited' friendship is made to bridge the prickly, opposing worlds of foemen. It is a lengthy depiction of the meeting of Diomedes, an Achaean, and Glaucus, son of Hippolochus. Diomedes immediately taunts his adversary, but adds that should he be a god he would not fight him. He then tells of how Lycurgus did not live long for striving with the gods. Diomedes proceeds to challenge Glaucus to enter the fray. Before engaging Diomedes the son of Hippolochus reflects on the ephemeral nature of human life, comparing the generations of man to leaves that are scattered by the wind, only to be replaced by the next generation in the cycle of the seasons. He then adds that he is descended from Bellerophon whose story he next relates. Bellerophon, falsely accused of making advances to Anteia, wife of King Proteus, was sent away to Anteia's father in Lycia, with baneful tokens that were to ensure he be killed. Bellerophon was assigned a number of dangerous tasks which were to bring him down, but which he instead accomplished. The King recognized that Bellerophon was not guilty and offered the hand of his daughter, as well as an orchard and plough-land. To this couple was born Hippolochus, father of Glaucus.

It is with gladness in his heart that Diomedes responds, as he thrusts his spear deep into the soil. It turns out that Oeneus, father of Diomedes, entertained the peerless Bellerophon in his halls for twenty days. Before parting ways, they exchanged gifts of friendship. Homer then returns his audience to the battlefield where Diomedes and Glaucus were sworn enemies locked in battle. However, all has changed as a result of the friendship of one's grandfather and the other's father. They now declare their own guest-friendship, and their intent to shun one another's spears. The two warriors then exchange armour, for all to see that they are friends from their fathers' days. The pledge of friendship is then sealed by Diomedes and Glaucus in a final gesture – they leap from their chariots and clasp one anothers' hands.

Virgil found Menno's account astounding, and the passion with which he delivered it, especially his emphasis on friendship (φιλία) that wards off the toil of destruction. An alternative world is found in the midst of slaughter, a place of consciousness where spears can be put aside. A friendship from a past era is able to safeguard Diomedes and Glaucus, each from the other. The friendship is pledged anew for their generation. It is accompanied by gentle words and gladness of heart. The retribution brought by friendship is something else; it is concord—the same as mercy shown the suppliant, an outcome when a life is saved, strife avoided, and where a qualified harmony surfaces, if only for a moment on the larger canvas of battle.

In Book VII Homer again draws attention to a similar instance where 'soul-devouring strife' is averted through a compact of friendship. In this scene a belt of bright scarlet is exchanged for a silver-studded sword. The declaration of friendship is between the larger-than-life heroes of the Trojan war, Hector and Ajax. And here as well the retribution of friendship is concord.

A further scene is similarly instructive, where an alternative to strife is provided. It is the meeting between King Priam of Troy and Achilles, who has destroyed so many lives. The picture painted here stands in contrast to the despoliation of beauty revealed in such detail in such a large part of the poem.

Here Homer draws attention to the role of compassion.

Priam has come to collect the body of his son Hector, whom Achilles had slain. What follows is the delineation of the tragedy of the war within the nature of Achilles, and that of man, to embody a capacity for mercy. As illustrated elsewhere, Achilles is the unyielding warrior, blinded by wrath, destructive of all in his path. And yet, he can be the paradigm of compassion and gentleness and understanding. It is the tragedy of man that both wrath and mercy dwell within him, as it can within one family, and in one city.

Homer's narrative begins with Priam's safe delivery across the darkness of the plain and past the enemy posts, courtesy of the god Hermes. Priam is guided directly to the hut of Achilles. What Priam does next is essentially what was done by the suppliant on the battlefield. He clasped in his hands the knees of Achilles, he kissed his hands, the man-slaying hands that had killed his son Hector, and so many of his sons. A far-reaching spirit of magnanimity follows in the story recalled of a man who through blindness has come upon a countryman and killed him – the killer then having to flee to a land of strangers, to a house of substance, where the one fleeing is looked upon with wonder. Similarly, Achilles was taken with wonder at the sight of godlike Priam, and likewise the old man was seized by wonder at the sight of Achilles. In such manner they beheld one another. The scene has begun with the astonishing gesture of Priam kissing Achilles' hands, an act which allows them to see beauty in one another.

The old man then requests, as he had been counselled, that Achilles might remember his own father, who was of the same age as Priam, on the threshold of grievous old age. Both fathers will be left with no one to care for them nor protect them, to ward off ruin. Priam continues by reminding Achilles of how much he has suffered, the loss of fifty sons, nineteen from one mother. Ares, the god of war has brought them down.

After his appeal to Achilles—to find commonality in the midst of war—he announced that he has come for the body of Hector and would willingly pay a ransom. Priam beseeches Achilles to stand in awe of the gods, to take pity on him, and to remember his own father, who is like Priam. Homer then returns his audience to the earlier moment when Priam offered what no other human could, as suppliant before the one who killed his sons. The entire scene is noteworthy for its depiction of the bare bones of the experience of war—the humbling loss of what matters in life, for all participants on the battlefield, and their loved ones!

Achilles nudges Priam with his hand, and the men proceed to weep, Priam for Hector, Achilles for his father Peleus and also for Patroclus. Achilles now pities the grey-silver head of the old man and raises him by the hand. He acknowledges the old man's valour and advises they put aside their sorrows, but not before the bitterness, referred to by Weil, is given full voice. The gods have thus set out the path for mortals: that they should live in pain, while they remain without sorrow. There are two urns at Zeus' feet, one of ills, the other of blessings. Some people get some from both, and some are given only ills and are driven mad over the face of the earth, being honoured by neither man nor god. Peleus and Priam were given glorious gifts, and now the slaying of their sons. The fathers of the foemen – Hector and Achilles – are united in their sorrowful fates.

During the accord which is brief and fragile Achilles' handmaids wash and anoint Hector's body with oil in preparation for its return to Priam. Reference is here made to Niobe for she was weary of shedding tears for her twelve slain children, and gave in to taking food. Priam is to follow Niobe's way and take food as well. When they have finished eating, again each marvelled at the beauty in the other, how comely and like the gods was Achilles, and what a vessel of excellence was Priam. On this note, not only of seeing the goodness in the other, but in the other who is also the foeman, Priam departs for his fair bed of purple blankets and fleecy coats to ensure his warmth. They are in agreement that there will be no combat for nine days to allow for Hector's funeral.

Achilles clasps the old man's hand by the wrist in a way more reminiscent of comrades' behaviour – perhaps more like the clasping of another's wrist during a light-stepping dance at a feast. Priam then leaves behind the light to retreat through the darkness with his son's body.

Homer's epic describes the price of battle not only by focusing on heroes like Hector, but in dozens of portraits – eleven of which will follow. In many of these we are given the familial context or background of those lost on the battlefield.

In Book IV, Ajax, son of Telamon, slays Simoeisius, son of Anthemion. Homer's sketch includes the past when the youth was born next to the River Simoeis, as his mother travelled with her parents to see their flocks below Mount Ida. But he did not pay back his parents for his upbringing. Instead, the span of his life was brief. Ajax's spear went straight through his breast and shoulder. Simoeisius fell to the dust like a poplar tree that had grown up on marshland, felled by a wainwright used in the construction of a chariot. Simoeisius' father's name, Anthemion, denotes that which buds like a flower. But his son will not go beyond the stage of budding to full flowering.

In Book V, 69-75, Pedaeus, son of Antenor was slain by Meges. He was a bastard in the technical sense of the term, and he was reared by Theano to please her husband as though he was one of her own children. He was struck by the spear on the sinew of the head, through his teeth, cutting off his tongue. The death of Pedaeus removes Homer's audience from the battlefield for a moment and is given all the more pathos by focusing on his mother. The sacrifice she made did not save his life, and yet her presence in the *Iliad* stands in contrast to the strife all around.

In Book VI, 12-19, Homer describes an attribute of the warrior slain. Diomedes slays Axylus, Teuthras' son, who dwelled in Arisbe. He was a man of substance, loved by all as he gave entertainment to all. Those who loved him were not there to save him from the foe. Like Theano, he is remembered for his generosity. Those who show generosity die along with their squire – in this case – the driver of his chariot.

In Book VIII, 302-08, Teucer strikes Gorgythion with an arrow through the breast. He was the son of Priam and a woman he wed from Aesyme. She was the fair Castianeira, in beauty and form like the goddesses. As he died, he bowed his head from the weight of the helmet, like a poppy in the rains of spring, laden with its fruit. The delicate and vulnerable beauty of flower and mother are brought forth in the poet's depiction: an illustration of the despoliation of beauty and the life of a mother's son.

In Book XI, 241-47, Agamemnon brutally kills Iphidamas, another son of Antenor. He was nurtured in deep-soiled Thrace by Cisseus who attempted to keep the youth from going to Troy by offering the youth the hand of his daughter, but the new bridegroom joined the Achaeans nonetheless. Homer here draws attention to the bride left behind. Iphidamas died in his youth, leaving behind a wife of whom he had yet known no joy. For his bride he had given a hundred kine and thereafter a thousand goats and sheep – herds past counting. In battle the value of the youth and his bride cannot be measured, as they are to no avail.

In Book XI, 324-25 Homer recounts the background of two warriors from the land of Apaesus and surrounding area. They were Adrastus and Amphius, sons of Merops of Percote. The father was highly skilled in prophecy and forbade his sons to go into war, the bane of men. But the two sons would not obey, as they were being led by the fates of black death. These warriors were robbed of their spirit and life by Diomedes, who fell upon them as wild boars upon hunting hounds. And so, their father's care and prophecy could not save them.

In Book XIII, 363-73, Diomedes takes the life of Othryoneus of Cabesus. He had just arrived to assist the Trojans and asked for the hand of the loveliest of King Priam's daughters, that of Cassandra. He had no gifts to offer but promised the mighty deed of driving the Achaeans from the Trojan plain. The warrior made a promise that he could not keep because he was blind to his own fate. What follows is the mockery of the dead man by Idomeneus of Crete. Othryoneus would go to war to get a bride, but it is in going to war that he loses his bride.

Again, in Book XIII, 428-33, Homer's audience is removed from the battlefield. Idomeneus slays Alcathous who had married the eldest daughter of Anchises, Hippodameia. She was heartily loved by her parents, her father and queenly mother. Their daughter excelled in her handiwork and her wisdom. And thus, the best man in Troy took her for his wife. The excellence of Hippodameia is here the subject Homer draws us to, and Alcathous' goodness is delineated by virtue of his connection to this excellence. Happiness in these halls is transformed and Hippodameia, who was heartily loved by her parents, is left to mourn the loss of her husband.

Elsewhere, in Book XV, 641-52, Hector slays Periphetes, the dear son of Copreus. Unfortunately, Periphetes tripped on the shield that reached down to his feet. He stumbled on it and fell backward as his helmet rang wondrously about him. Hector was quick to take notice of his vulnerability and struck him in the breast with his spear, as his dear comrades looked on, unable to come to his aid.

The poet notes that Periphetes was better in all manner of excellence, in doing battle, in fleetness of foot, and of mind. He was first among the men of Mycenae. The portrait underlines that such men are claimed by strife just as easily, and may occur in as senseless a fashion as tripping on one's own shield. There is meaninglessness in such a waste of excellence, a theme reiterated throughout Homer's poem.

In Book XX, 407-18, the narrative brings the audience to the fate of Polydorus. He was the youngest son of Priam whom his father would not suffer to fight in the war. Polydorus was godlike, the dearest in his father's eyes, and one who was unsurpassed in fleetness of foot. In foolishness, the youth ran among the warriors, to demonstrate his gift of running, albeit unarmed. As he ran past Achilles the swift-footed Achilles cast his spear and struck the youth in the back where the golden clasps of his belt were fastened, and darkness enfolded him. Priam wished to save his dearest son from the bane of war, but to no avail as he too is slain. Here is depicted the sorrow of the father, and the prevalence of a guiltless victim suffering the woes that are not his own. Polydorus died making a show of his excellence. He misjudged, his excellence could not save him; his name, Polydorus, means 'many-gifted'.

*

These portraits fascinated Menno. For him, the poet was purposeful in taking his audience to a place beyond the death of the warrior. There we are invited to consider the cost of war, mostly in terms of relationships (i.e., what this death meant for a mother, a father, a wife, an infant). As brief as the portraits are, they are remarkably poignant and effective in making his audience recall all that is central to a good life, beyond valour and the feats of heroes.

When Patroclus, 'θεράπων' of Achilles, is slain he was shielded by Achilles' armour which he had worn to strike fear in the hearts of the enemy. The captive young woman, fought over by King Agamemnon and Achilles – the beautiful Briseis – was in Patroclus' charge when he was killed. She has already lost her husband and three brothers to the Achaeans, and for kind Patroclus she will mourn more.

With the death of Patroclus, Achilles is prepared to put aside his wrath for King Agamemnon. Homer describes Achilles' change of heart. He confesses that strife should perish among gods and men, and anger should perish that makes a man wrathful. Wrath – wrath that is sweet as trickling honey, that spreads like smoke in the breast of man – is the poet's focus. He has led his audience from weeping and suffering to an awareness of the pervasiveness and futility of 'soul-devouring strife.' He moves further toward an awareness that vengeance will go on and on, circling back to even more tears and mourning. Before Patroclus' death, at the time that the Trojans are slaughtering Achaeans at the doorstep of their camp, Achilles is without pity. As Patroclus shed tears over those comrades lost, Achilles accuses him of being a child, like a girl that runs to her mother's side to be picked up.

Patroclus replies with cutting words; he wishes that he would never be held in the grip of wrath. Achilles' valour is a bane to the Argives. Indeed, Achilles is pitiless; his father is not the knight Peleus, nor is the nymph Thetis his mother, but the grey sea and the beetling cliffs gave birth to him! He is as unbending as the laws of nature.

All human beings, like Achilles, face a choice: to bend our hearts or to forgive is within the potential of all humans, in place of giving in to vengeance. Menno ended his outdoor lesson for Virgil by boldly suggesting that if there were a beginning point of religion it could be found in Patroclus' striking words. People are given the potential to reach beyond the world where causes are regarded as external to the will. Virgil politely asked if he could say a few words.

'I want to say what you have heard before, that this is not a true story, and that all these gods are not approachable – not to my understanding, and certainly not as they are presented as active participants in the carnage. I admit that there could be a relation between friendship and love. Seeing the other person in yourself and the appeal to mercy – these are not outside a life of faith as I see it. The examples of how suffering in war cannot be contained, that the victor also suffers, if differently – these together invite consideration. Maybe you and Simone Weil are on to something.'

'And maybe I should delay my journey to Athos, and instead join you on Samos.' Menno had a brief moment to wonder how he knew that he was going to Samos, before Virgil interrupted his line of thought. 'Along our way I could tell you about my acquaintance with Bishop Ireneos of Crete.'

They agreed to meet the next morning, Menno with no small degree of reluctance. But before returning to his room Menno stopped at a taverna for dinner. It was late in the evening and the citizens of Chios were in a celebratory mood. Tables had been pushed aside and a circle dance was in progress, likely the dance known as the Kalamatianos. It was a popular dance, one with roots going back to antiquity, and one where the participants danced in a circle while holding hands.

Menno observed the dance with great interest. As a Canadian of Joni Mitchell's generation he recalled the lyrics from her song "The Circle Game:" 'We can't return we can only look behind, from where we came, and go round and round and round, in the circle game' More importantly the setting brought him back to Homer. In Book XVIII, 590-620, Homer describes the shield for Achilles fashioned by Hephaestus. On the shield Homer delivered his audience to a place of peace, far from the battlefield, to a well wrought dancing floor. Here young people are dancing, holding their hands upon the wrists of the next dancer. And they ran lightly round, and in rows toward each other holding hands. Both the memory of the shield of Achilles and the scene before him in the taverna brought back memories from Menno's youth when he enjoyed a similar entertainment, another circle dance (likely adopted in the Ukraine) known as 'metelytsia.' At the same time Menno was called back to the holding of hands that defined the sacred truce at Olympia. He concluded that there was likely no better emblem of peace than the holding of hands.

The next morning as Menno returned to the port of Chios, he considered whether it was here, or at Smyrna, or elsewhere that Homer was born. Perhaps these things did not matter. Not next to the poet's gift to the world. Besides, he would not have time alone to ponder such questions. There was Virgil waiting at the harbour, although Menno did not recall issuing an invitation for him to join him.

Samos-Pythagorio

Pythagoras

After a delay of a few hours, Menno and Virgil boarded the next ferry southward for Samos. On the upper deck in a brisk breeze Virgil described his trip to Crete. He told Menno how Bishop Ireneos had invited the relief organization MCC to begin a program on the Island of Crete. The program provided supplies beginning in 1961, with some going to Orthodox hostels. A vocational school and demonstration centre were established for local farmers, offering helpful animal husbandry and beekeeping instruction for enhancing production.

MCC was still there, and Virgil had been able to meet with staff and farmers. In his encounters he found that a most interesting relationship between the locals and the MCC volunteers had evolved. Because of the trust that had grown over the years, they were considering continuing a dialogue even after the departure of MCC workers. Virgil thought that more than one bridge had been built between two churches, and between two cultures.

Upon hearing this, Menno's thoughts moved along to an indistinct character in Greek history, one with a disproportionate influence on the centuries that followed. Again, Menno explained for the benefit of Virgil that Pythagoras was that most enigmatic figure in archaic Greece.[9] His teachings penetrated so many fields of Greek life, from poetry and philosophy, to architecture and science. Two centuries later his mark was left on Plato, whom Aristotle considered a Pythagorean. The roots of his thought reach back to Sumeria and Egypt from whom the Pythagoreans had assimilated many ideas, according to Herodotus.

Pythagoras was born at Samos in about 560 BCE, or possibly raised there after being brought from Phoenicia, where his father was a trader. He likely left Samos around the year 532, possibly to escape the politics of Samos' tyranny at the time. He then sailed to the South of present day Italy, to Croton, an area densely populated by earlier Greek colonies. Here he established his academy.

Upon arrival at Vathy, on the north shore of the Island of Samos, Menno enquired about buses that cross the island to Pythagorio, the capital in antiquity. The bus came close to but did not stop at the once prominent Temple of Hera reconstructed a few times before the gigantic structure built by Polycrates in the second half of the sixth century BCE.

Along the way, the bus ride provided its own entertainment. The bus driver appeared to know all the villagers along his route. There was plenty of beeping to greet farmers working in the fields next to the road. One unannounced stop resulted in a business transaction where eggs were brought on board in return for jars of olive oil being exchanged. At another stop Menno was delighted to witness a young lad being delivered to the care of the driver, after a very lively conversation. The driver now offered childcare in addition to driving to Pythagorio. Menno noticed that the unexpected entertainment along the way revealed relationships within communities that were still whole.

After being left in Pythagorio, Menno acquired a map that led them to the famous tunnel of Eupalinos of Megara, built around the time that Pythagoras abandoned Samos. The tunnel was built as an aqueduct that would deliver water to the ancient capital over a distance of a kilometre. It was at the time only the second known tunnel that was begun from both ends at the same time, and that successfully met in the middle. It would remain in use for over a thousand years.

As Menno and Virgil hiked back to Pythagorio, Menno recalled another noteworthy islander born on Samos; namely, Aristarchus (310-230 BCE) who proposed the first known heliocentric model of the planets. He placed the sun at the centre with the earth revolving around it. He too studied in Egypt, at Alexandria. Repeatedly, it seems the inhabitants of this Asia Minor coastal region benefited from the accomplishments and advancements of older and larger civilizations, like that of Egypt. They would go on to build on the earlier discoveries and learning, as in geometry for example. Pythagoras was likely given similar advantage.

Exhausted from their hike, they found a seat that beckoned along the ancient mole. There Menno removed from his backpack the notes on Pythagoras he had brought along. For the benefit of Virgil he read aloud the few sources for the enigmatic philosopher – bits on scraps of paper copied from Philolaus, an early disciple, and excerpts from Philebus, Epinomis, and the *Gorgias* and *Timaeus* of Plato.

Pittakos was nearing the end of his life when Pythagoras was born. Apparently, Thales was yet of vigorous mind so that he could offer Pythagoras instruction, among other things to visit Egypt, where according to some accounts he spent a good deal of time. Nonetheless, the disposition of the seven sages is readily seen in Pythagoras' thought as well. There is a profound dis-ease with the prevalence of strife, conflict and discord in archaic Greece. For Pythagoras, what was missing was harmony, and a form of harmony inseparable from that which is just and beautiful. And the practice of philosophy was the remedy for discord; it was the means of spiritual purification that would lead the soul to its destiny: union with the divine.

A central idea of the Pythagoreans is that of the metaphysic of number. All of reality, including music, astronomy, the health of the human body, as that of the city-state, is at its base mathematical in nature. Pythagoras began with music and number, and through that portal viewed the world he lived in. Through number Pythagoras could perceive the beautifully ordered cosmos. For him, the essential principle for phenomenal reality was that matter (the indefinite) was shaped by Form (that which has limit). In this way to his mind multiplicity and unity were joined. It was a penchant of Greek thought, over the centuries, to make sense of the apparent multiplicity in life and to seek unity in its place. The tetraktys (ten points, with one on the top of a triangle and four at the bottom) was for Pythagoras the paradigm of whole systems; it linked the dimensionless to oneness; it contained and revealed the symphonic ratios which underlie the mathematical harmony of the musical scale: 1:2 (octave), 2:3 (perfect fifth), and 3:4 (perfect fourth)!

Altogether, this awareness stemming from the discovery of musical intervals led to his philosophy of αναλογία, analogy. Thereby number accounted for other phenomena in the cosmic order, beyond tone and music; namely, planetary motion and the music of the spheres, health in the human body seen as the perfect harmony of the elements comprising the body (as in Hippocratic medicine), and as proportion underlies the health of the soul, so justice underlies the orderly city-state. This is so wherein the laws set by lawgivers, often sages, reflect the harmony of universal laws in evidence in the cosmos.

For Pythagoras, because universal principles could be revealed to the human mind, assimilation to these, or to god, was possible through philosophy. This was possible because human beings are a microcosm, a compendium of the universe, one that contains the powers and attributes of the cosmos. Individuals were seen as a world order in miniature, embracing the same principles. So, the challenge for an individual was one of becoming aware of the divine universal principles already within (cf. John 1:12: all who received Jesus were children of God). It is for this reason that Pythagoras did not seek to transcend or disengage from the material world. Rather, the goal was to exist within the cosmos, one that was divinely beautiful, with awareness of our intellect's potential. The goal was to enhance the function, through awareness, of the transcendent harmony in the natural and social orders. Because divinity was immanent (as in the statement by Thales: 'all things are full of the gods') in the cosmos it followed that contemplation of divine laws (philosophy) was at the same time contact with the divine! In other words, the very Logos of relationship spelled out that every part has its place in the total fabric, thereby ensuring the unity of the whole. Pythagoras' approach integrates the disciplines of mathematics, psychology, medicine, ethics and political philosophy into one comprehensive whole. That is, philosophy and science had not yet been divorced.

In daily life, Pythagoras advocated for a life of asceticism that included a contempt for fame and wealth. Living with less was in keeping with the maxim 'nothing in excess,' the Delphic injunction also advocated by the seven sages.

While the Semitic heritage also boasted a number of ascetics, it did not as clearly rule out wealth as a reward, as in Proverbs 10:22, 'The blessing of the Lord brings wealth without painful toil for it.' Moreover, in

Pythagoras' view, living with less would have the same positive effect as the pursuit of music. Both would perform a sort of soul adjustment leading from a clear vision of life. It followed that the most just behaviour or practice was to sacrifice—to give something of oneself.

In the words of Kenneth Clark: "in order to free the spirit we must shed all our earthly goods... It is an ideal to which, however impossible it may be in practice, the finest spirits will always return."

The most excellent thing was that which follows soul adjustment: namely, felicity. For Pythagoras friendship, 'φιλία', figured largely as a part of the excellence of felicity. Pythagoras attended the Olympic Games in 528 BC. He taught that the Games by mutual association should transform hostility into friendship, and friendship was essentially equality. A friend was another self. Thus there was to be universal amity of all to all. No harm was to be done to animals, and no animals were to be sacrificed. He believed that if you see the slaughter of animals as iniquitous, you will see killing a man more unlawful, as was engagement in war.

For Menno these teachings were astonishing as they were coincident with his Anabaptist heritage, with the significant exception that animals could be killed and consumed. Friendship could be more readily cultivated in the presence of justice, as justice was in essence mutuality and equality. Like the union of soul and body, it was a relationship of cooperation. Moreover, justice would ensure the increase in things held in common and be enhanced by association. This way of understanding extended to the management of the household; to be done with less, and underlined with temperance. This ought to proceed through legislative means that would have preventative and didactic effects. For Pythagoras, equity had to be the sign of good laws that permeate the soul and habits of the citizens. Equity of this nature could not feed privilege, but should ensure the sick and suffering are cared for. In introducing legislation lawgivers were not to lose sight of the maxim of justice: 'touch not the balance above the beam,' or, do not disturb the divine universal order. Menno thought that balance was the same as equilibrium in Greek. Ροπή referred to the balance of the scales, when equally matched you created an equilibrium, or ισορροπία.

Pythagoras' way of philosophy is centred on care for the soul, as the soul itself is harmony. By giving attention to the principle of harmony, expressed by number and proportion in the external world, we can activate the same within the microcosm that is within ourselves. Thus were found the words inscribed over the entrance of Plato's Academy: 'let no one ignorant of geometry enter here'.

For Pythagoras the end of philosophy was caring for the soul and assimilation with the gods. Here we see our place in the connected mosaic: a place that denotes an awakening to recognize the macrocosm, the universal presence that is divine within ourselves; a place where the symbol of number is understood as communication within the apparent multiplicity in life; a place not only of recognition of connectivity as a core attribute of our world, but of the parallel of this universal order in the microcosm.

A beginning point for Pythagoreans was the acknowledgment of error, of incompleteness in perception (both a form of hubris and humility). In a way, this is similar to confession. This acknowledgement recognizes the baneful recurrence of conflict and strife, of slaughter and destruction, of the unlawful nature of both killing and of war. This recurrence leads inevitably to the erasing of all that we live for, the beauty found in everyday life. This is the face of discord. Pherecydes of Syros was an influential teacher of Pythagoras'. He taught that when the cosmos was created, Eros appeared to bring opposites into harmony, and to extend likeness and unity through all things.

In order to awaken, we need to avoid surfeit; we need to practice the holding of possessions in common within communities. We are on the way to the philosophy of Pythagoras when we see this profound analogy in the connectivity between the universe as macrocosm and ourselves as microcosm. The image is pivotal in Pythagoras' thought; it is the bridge between 'there is something greater than I,' and the simultaneous greatness at the centre of what constitutes the individual.

For Menno, this way of thinking was familiar because he had read the Gospel of John in particular. Immanence was in evidence in Jesus Christ as the eternal Logos; the Divine principle by whose agency the operative intelligence of God is manifested and made effective throughout the universe.

The following examples are clear in this regard. John 6:53, "Verily, verily I say unto you, Except ye eat the flesh of the son of man, and drink his blood, ye have no life in you." John 15:4, "Abide in me and I in you. As the branch cannot bear fruit of itself, except it abides in the vine; no more can ye, except ye abide in me." John 17:23, "I in them, and thou in me, that they may be made perfect in one; and that the world may know that thou hast sent me, and hast loved them, as thou hast loved me." And 1 John 4:15, "Whosoever shall confess that Jesus is the son of God, God dwelleth in him, and he in God." It seemed to Menno that the microcosm-macrocosm model in Pythagoras was not at all far removed from the principle of immanence in the Gospel of John—indeed an almost seamless progression from the ancients.

For Pythagoras, philosophy was incapable of separating itself from the harmonies of music, from caring for the sick and dispossessed, from abstinence from violence and the taking of another's life. In spirit, the Pythagoreans were largely in keeping with what we know of the seven sages. When we see the beauty in the microcosm, in our fellow person, thoughts of revenge are usurped and displaced by reconciliation. Indeed, in Matthew 5: 44-45 "Christ said, love your enemies, bless them that curse you, do good to them that hate you, and pray for them that despitefully use you and persecute you, that ye may be children of your Father in heaven." When we see with other eyes, we see the other in ourselves, and ourselves connected to all. In such a world we can see that disease is to the health of the body what ignorance is to the soul, and what discord is to the well-being of the city-state.

While it is not possible to reliably ascribe certain thoughts to Pythagoras, the aforementioned approx.-imations of his views have some consistency among sources, albeit late ones known to us. In the end it is fair to say that the Pythagoreans were remembered for fostering health and harmony, as in the example of Hippocrates. They advocated for justice and equity, celebrated the friendship of all for all, and they would be especially remembered for arbitrating disputes and promoting mutual assistance.

While the crucial role of philosophy in caring for one's soul was not a part of Menno's heritage, nor was equating beauty with justice, he found familiarity in the confession of failure in our human relationships, and in the foremost need to overcome strife that seems ubiquitous. For disagreement and discord were central to humanity's missing the mark ('ἁμαρτία', the Greek word for sin). Seeking harmony and concord through equity, caring for those in need, through the arbitration of disputes and mutual life – all of these seemed very much in accord with Menno's heritage. After all, peacemaking, arbitrating disputes, and the principle of non-resistance were a core part of the foundation of Menno's heritage.

For example, at about the time Menno returned to Greece for further studies, Project Ploughshares was being launched at Conrad Grebel College and exhort-ations to be of service to your fellow person, as in mutual aid and the relief work of the Mennonite Central Committee, were at one with the way of this enigmatic philosopher, Pythagoras.

For Pythagoras, the way to union with god passed through reincarnations until human beings got it right. But in their conversations, Virgil was quick to point out that such ideas did not receive ready approval among most Mennonites. But Menno was ready for him. He reminded Virgil there were indeed hints of reincarnation in the Gospels. In Matthew 16, 13-16, Jesus asks his disciples, "who do they say that I am?" He was then told that some people thought he was Elijah, others that he was John the Baptist, yet others that he was Jeremias. But Peter declares that he is the son of the living God.

Before Virgil left, he confessed that the teachings of Pythagoras had made him wonder about the years following Jesus resurrection. In order to understand these years, it seemed important to be aware of the Greek contribution. As a youth he had read of the highly variegated beginnings of the Christian movement. There was disagreement on the degree to which the Jewish law of the Torah was to be observed. Paul emphasized the coming of salvation through the death and resurrection of Jesus. The gnostics underlined, as revealed in the Nag Hammadi literature, the importance of wisdom, knowledge, the teachings and message of Jesus. In Rome alone we find Justin Martyr in a separate school from the gnostic teacher Valentinus, and Marcion who would proclaim that the God of the New Testament was not the same God as the Old Testament. In time, the latter would be declared a heretic. But to little effect, during the first centuries when there was a proliferation of gospels.

Menno interrupted,

'Yes, I agree, Paul is writing to followers in Ephesus, Philippi, Corinth, and Thessaloniki to ensure the unanimity of their beliefs. There is debate and disagreement on too many fronts. In the end they focused on what should identify a person as a follower of Jesus. That translated into what one believed, and depended greatly on where the source of authority lay. And if you did not fit into the nascent mainstream, you were declared a heretic (from the Greek, αἱρεσις, originally signifying a choice different from the majority view). We should be reminded that even though Marcion was expelled from the church in 144 CE, the movement still became more widespread.'

Virgil left, after little more comment, which was unexpected. He seemed to be engrossed in thought. Yet, he managed to say that much appealed to him about Pythagoras. However, for him philosophy could never replace the Anointed One. He thought, knowing what Menno had been taught, Menno should not accept that either. It was not an unfriendly parting of ways, but Menno felt some relief that Virgil would be making his way to Mount Athos while he went on to Piraeus without his critic.

Thebes

Sophocles

Upon resting after an arduous, rather windy, passage between Vathy and Piraeus, Menno was determined to visit the Boeotian city of Thebes. A three-hour interrupted bus ride from the busy terminal in Athens brought him to the legendary city founded by the Phoenician Cadmus. It's first founder, who had come from the Near East City of Tyre, was the brother of Europa, once abducted by Zeus himself, and according to Herodotus, he was the one who introduced the Phoenician script that would over time form the basis of the Greek alphabet (after Minoan Linear A and Linear B writing).

Thebes was the birthplace of Pindar, an outstanding lyric poet who was born after Pythagoras died. He may have met Philolaus, a disciple of Pythagoras, who moved to Thebes after many Pythagoreans were killed and driven from southern Italy. Philolaus is alleged to have brought the teachings of Pythagoras to Thebes. In Pindar's poetry there are only glimpses of the social crises of the archaic period — from the backdrop of the founding of innumerable colonies to relieve overpopulation and limited land resources to the privilege of the aristocratic class. Pindar's interest and focus was the celebration of Olympian victors, and this he expressed through his Epinician odes.[10] Pindar praises athletes of several city-states by lauding their openness to strangers. The poet suggests keeping one's distance from pride and surfeit, and one's heart above possessions.

> '(Apollo) brings to the heart
> Law, that thinks not of battle...'

And battle is not a pretty thing, as illustrated in the legend of the seven against Thebes:

> 'And with their bodies they fattened
> The white flowers of smoke...
> Seven pyres feasted on young men's limbs.'
> (Nem IX)

And the alternative? With the gods' help:

'The man who leads them...
Shall give his people honour
And turn them to peaceful concord.'
(Pythian I)

And:

'Praise your enemy also
Who... in justice does well'.
(Pythian IX)

All to say that Pindar, born in c 518 BCE, carried forward a core piece of the tradition from Homer, Archilochus, the archaic sages, and Pythagoras — and that is the awareness of the tragic presence of discord in the world.

Menno may not have stopped at Thebes were it not for the playwright of tragedies, Sophocles. At the age of sixteen Sophocles led the choral-paean, celebrating the Greek victory over the Persians at the Battle of Salamis. He would in later life serve as Treasurer, Strategos (military leader), and as a proboulos (advisory commissioner). Yet his renown rests firmly on his dramatic work: over one hundred plays, and possibly as many as twenty-four victories in competitions, which is more than his worthy elder, Aeschylus, and younger fellow playwright Euripides.

Menno had brought with him a copy of Sophocles' play, *Antigone*.[11] In the preface to the play, which was translated by H. D. F. Kitto, the professor guides the reader to approach and understand the art of the playwright. For example, he emphasizes that, for the

Greeks, passion was more powerfully expressed by subjecting it to strict and formal control. Sophocles' plays are not about tragic heroes or tragic individuals, but they take place on the broader canvas of the human condition. Kitto also reminds his reader that Sophocles' actors are not puppets at the mercy of Omnipotence. Rather, the gods represent

> 'the immanent laws or conditions of human existence, those which we must obey or perish—in Antigone's case, obey and perish... and what we call life, what confronts us is so vast, so complex, that Man must not arrogantly suppose that he is in control and therefor need no longer respect the constraints of religion.'

The play tells the story of Cadmus' descendants, after the rule of King Laius, of King Oedipus, and Jocasta's children. One son – Eteocles – died defending Thebes (and his crown) from his brother Polyneices, who in turn was killed by Eteocles. Their uncle Creon, who inherited the crown, ordained that honour be shown to Eteocles along with every solemn funerary rite and ceremony. For Polyneices there was to be no funeral, let alone a burial. Rather, he is to provide a feast for wild birds and dogs. The brothers' one sister, Ismene, fears Creon's decree that anyone who would bury Polyneices would themselves be killed. The other sister, Antigone, feels that she will have to please the dead far longer than the living. She will bury her brother, in order not to dishonour the sacred laws of heaven. We are told that the brothers shared an unnatural hatred for one another, the two sons of one mother.

Antigone buries her brother, and then the chorus questions whether this might not be the 'hand of god,' adding that if a human being observes the Laws of heaven and treads the path of right that God ordained, he is honoured; the opposite follows if he joins hands with sin. After the guards remove the dirt from Polyneices' body, Antigone is caught in the act of burying the body for a second time. She pours a funeral libation before being delivered to King Creon. Her defence was that Zeus did not publish a decree that would prohibit the proper burial of her brother. The laws of heaven are unwritten and unchanging, and before the gods' tribunal she stands. Moreover, who knows if the brothers may not be reconciled in death? And then, she proclaims her deepest feelings in a line of the play that leapt off the page, surprising Menno:

> 'Even so, I give both love, not share their hatred,' or 'I cannot share in hate, but only in love' (συμφιλέω, to love mutually; συμφιλεῖν ἔφυν, born or raised to love). (l. 513)

She gives love to both of her brothers, but Creon responds that she will then go down to Hades. She can love there, if she must. But another reference to love appears in response to her sister's wish to join Antigone in her fate. Antigone makes it known that she does not wish to love those who love in words alone.

We then learn that Creon's son, Haemon, was supposed to marry Antigone. But Creon says that he hates a son to have an evil wife, and the chorus reflects on the ensuing events before ancient sorrows rise again; disaster linked to disaster. To the one whom God would ruin, evil seems good in his poor judgment. Haemon counsels his father to forego thinking that he alone is wise, to allow his anger to cool, to know when to yield, and to bend like the branches of trees. He reminds his father that the city is on Antigone's side and that the citizens find her fate most undeserved. He then declares he will die with Antigone, for Creon is opposing justice. This is implacable love and no one can escape its dominion, not against the invincible Aphrodite.

Tiresias, the seer of Thebes, enters late in the play. He announces that things have gone awry: sacrifices will not burn on the altars, sickness has come upon them, and the sacred hearths have been polluted by dogs and birds gorging on the body of Polyneices. Tiresias advises that the wise man should amend his ways, yield to the dead, and forbear to strike the fallen or slay the slain. He goes on to reveal what is about to happen. Creon will lose his son – death for death – as he has sentenced Antigone to a slow death imprisoned in a cavern. The chorus then confirms that Tiresias' prophecies have been fulfilled. It is too late when Creon determines to set Antigone free. He comes to his senses, but he is out of time. Creon loses Eurydice, his wife, as well. Indeed, the great are overthrown and the lowly are raised up. The path of wisdom appears too late. Creon was blinded. The chorus reiterates that wisdom is the greater part of happiness, and so is reverence towards the gods.

Menno could not put out of his mind the spirit of Antigone, and her will not to share in hate, but only in love. He wondered whether Melpomene, the muse of tragedy, was near at hand. Thebes was about twenty kilometres east of Mount Helicon, home of the muses and where the early archaic poet Hesiod was given his 'voice' by the muses. It was near Thespiae, in the Valley of the Muses, that a sanctuary of the muses could be found. An Ionic temple, the spring of Hippocrene once struck by the hoof of the winged horse Pegasus and an inspiration to poets, a theatre, statues of the muses, and a long stoa that housed votive offerings to the muses. These were all located in the sanctuary.

Mount Helicon was known for the Valley of the Muses, but also for the nearby home of Hesiod at Ascra. It happened also to be the place where Narcissus gazed into the pool of water in admiration of himself, before his transformation into a different beauty, that of the flower.

Fortunate for Menno, he was able to catch a ride with a farmer whom he had met in the market at Thebes. Past fields of maize, vineyards, and scrubland they progressed in an old Toyota truck that made occasionally discouraging coughing spurts. After an hour or so, Menno was deposited at the sanctuary where it required all of his imagination to conjure up what was once there in the fourth and third centuries. The foundations alone could not quite bring back the festivities that had occurred here. Nonetheless, before beginning his long trek back to Thebes, Menno retrieved from his backpack Hesiod's *Theogony* where the poet had sung of the muses:

> 'Let us begin our singing
> From the Heliconian muses who possess
> the great and holy
> Mountain of Helicon....'

and

> 'light are the feet they move on.'
> (ll. 1-8)[12]

These are the words of Hesiod, whom the muses found shepherding his lambs on Mount Helicon, who gave him a staff of olive shoot, 'and breathed a voice' into him. These are the muses:

> 'Who by their singing
> Delight the great mind of Zeus, their father.'
> (ll. 36-37)

Their mother Mnemosyne bore the nine in Pieria:

> 'She bore her nine daughters, concordant
> Of heart, and singing is all the thought
> that is in them
> And no care troubles their spirits.'
> (ll.60-61)

The voices of the muses play a role in the straight decisions of judges, putting an end to quarrels. Theirs are voices of gentle agreement that turn back in the right direction those who have gone astray. Their song allows the listeners to forget their cares.

'Such is the holy gift the muses give to humanity.'
(l. 93)

Menno lingered along the way, stopping to consider what Hesiod had to say about the muses. He walked half the way back to Thebes before being picked up by a kindly local priest who was fluent in English. During the ride back to Thebes, Menno shared his reason for returning to Greece and told him what the pilgrimage was all about. The priest listened intently, and after a few minutes of silence, he began:

'I understand – I think – the gist of your inspiration and enthusiasm for the ancient Greek world. Let me tell you about Clement of Alexandria. He was born around the year 150 after Christ and became a convert to the Christian faith, but not before being instructed in Greek philosophy. He went on to become a leader of the Christian community in Alexandria. For Clement, Greek philosophy served a similar role to law for the Jews. It was a necessary step in leading to the Truth, personified as Logos. That is, there was a kind of mosaic of traditions that precede and enter Christianity. There was one way of Truth, thought Clement, but several streams flowed into it. I think he saw that Greek philosophy prepared the world for Christianity. If I recall correctly, Clement was initiated into the Eleusinian mysteries, which is thought to have been reflected in his writings. Much in keeping with early Greek thought, he saw all Truth as one. In other and more contemporary words, the truths of secular science must be one with the truths of revelation. Clement – if I have remembered correctly – did not follow the Gnostics in discarding the Old Testament. Instead, he favoured a generous form of allegorical interpretation.

'And, of course, you might not know of Justin of Caesarea, or Justin Martyr. He was born before Clement, sometime around 100 after Christ. He too was an early Christian apologist who had been trained in Greek philosophy. If I understand correctly, he promoted the idea that the Logos was active in history, acting like seeds of Christianity before Christ's incarnate presence. This led him to think of ancient Greeks – like Socrates, Plato, and Heraclitus – as unknowing Christians.

'Now the later Church was not always receptive to these early ideas. But you might discover sympathetic souls in the first centuries; others like Clement and Justin. Views that might not be so different from yours. I would not discourage you from continuing on your path, and certainly not for continuing to seek Truth.'

For Menno, the priest's words were wonderfully uplifting. Upon parting ways in Thebes, Menno thanked him for his insights, and the priest smiled and added, 'You should know that I don't always speak for everyone in my Church.'

Sparta

Archaeological Site of Ancient Sparta

Menno had decided to return to Athens the following morning where he transferred to a bus that then took him to Sparta, in lovely Laconia. Fringed on the west by Mount Taygetus and on the east by Mount Parnon was the valley of the River Eurotos on the west bank of which is the city of Sparta. Already in the eighth century BCE Sparta had made war on Messenia and in victory had annexed most of their territory. The vanquished population, known as helots, were coerced to farm land for the Spartans. To ensure that the helots did not revolt the famous socio-military institutions that Sparta became known for, were set in place: a deadening form of military training, where young men were removed from their parents at a young age and forced into militaristic obedience. King Lycurgus was given credit for implementing this militaristic way of life. Much later, at the end of the Peloponnesian war, in 404 BCE, Sparta defeated Athens. About thirty years later Spartan supremacy came to an end after the Battle of Leuctra and the restoration of Messenian independence.

One of Sparta's well known poets was Tyrtaeus, whose elegies propped up the military state. His poetry centred on exhortations to support the authority of the city-state, and he enjoined his readers to fight bravely to the end — until victory or death. He encouraged them to engage in battle in close hand-to-hand combat in order to take the enemy's life. Indeed, Spartan honour required coming home carrying your shield, or being carried on it, dead. The Battle of Thermopylae, during the second invasion of Greece by Persian forces (this time by Xerxes) was a never-to-be forgotten tribute to Spartan courage. Led by King Leonidas, the Spartans held the road that blocked the Persian advance for several days – all three hundred of them giving their lives to do so!

On the burial mound at Thermopylae, an epitaph recorded the following:

> Stranger, who passes by
> go tell the Spartans
> that here, obedient to their laws
> we lie.

Chilon of Sparta, another of the seven sages, lived circa 600 BCE.[13] He was honoured in Sparta as a hero, mostly for his political contributions, and as a wise man. He was thus made an ephor, or counsellor, to the king. He was credited with the development of the Peloponnesian League in the sixth century, and according to legend, he died of joy at Olympia when his son won the prize for boxing at the Games.

Diogenes Laertius, in his *Lives and Opinions of the Eminent Philosophers*, attributes a number of maxims and sayings to Chilon. People are not to speak evil of the dead. It is best to prefer punishment to disgraceful gain, as the latter will cast its shadow for the remainder of one's life. He suggests that we should not mock or laugh at someone for their misfortune. It is better to be respected than feared, so mercy is best shown if one is strong. His readers are counselled to honour old age, to obey the laws, and importantly, to restrain anger.

In his reply to Aesop, Chilon is alleged to have answered the question of what Zeus is doing — humbling the proud and exalting the humble. Chilon advised not to abuse one's neighbours and to be more ready to visit friends in adversity than in prosperity. In a city-state that ruled the Helots through coercion and fear, Chilon appears in contrast with his countrymen, especially the poet Tyrtaeus. On the other hand, he is – unsurprisingly – very much in agreement with the counsel of his fellow sages.

Epidauros

Asklepios
Epidauros Archaeological Museum

Menno left the land of Chilon, Tyrtaeus, and Lycurgus, and travelled – again by bus – through Tripolis to Nauplion. There he connected by bus to Epidauros. He had a few hours in Nauplion before the next bus departed for Epidauros. Menno took the time to climb the outcrop of rock on which the Palamidi fortress was built by the Venetians in the early 18th century. The outcrop was named for Palamedes, son of Nauplios, who accompanied the Achaeans to Troy. While at Troy, so the story goes, Palamedes was falsely accused of treason and put to death. The wiley Odysseus was behind the plot.

After ascending the nine hundred plus steps to the summit, and being considerably out of breath, Menno asked a stranger if there was a shop up there that sold water. It appeared there was not. A young gentleman overheard the exchange, approached, and handed him a small bottle of water. In the conversation that followed the young man said that his name was Willems, that he was from the Netherlands, and that he taught high school literature. He added that there was a play written about Palamedes that he taught his class.

Menno was intrigued and asked about the play. Willems was happy to oblige. The playwright was Joost van den Vondel, who was born in Cologne in 1587, of Mennonite parents, who had left Antwerp and moved to Amsterdam after Joost was born. As an adult, the poet and playwright belonged to the Waterlander Mennonites, who were known to be less strict, more liberal, and open to the world.

At a later date he joined the Catholic Church, but was thought to have retained convictions from his Mennonite past. Willems claimed that Van den Vondel was considered to be the most important Dutch playwright of the 17th century. The Palamedes play was one of thirty-three plays that he wrote, and when it was put on the stage in 1625 it was read as an allegory of the 1619 execution of the Advocate of Holland. It was a false accusation, an injustice that was dealt to Palamedes a very long time earlier. Menno was thrilled to have met Willems and told him so. He was familiar with the legend of Palamedes, but had not even heard of van den Vondel, nor had he known of the existence of a Mennonite in the 17th century who had shown an interest in ancient Greece, and who had studied ancient Greek! Through a brief fortuitous encounter Menno felt his confidence swelling. Perhaps he was not altogether alone in his convictions.

The much-visited archaeological site was a short, pleasant bus ride through the storied Argolid, with glimpses of a few Mycenaean bridges in evidence in a few ravines. For perhaps a millennium Epidauros was the premier healing sanctuary of several sites dedicated to the god of medicine, Asklepios. At the same time the site hosted athletic, dramatic, and musical competitions every four years in honour of the god. To celebrate the gods, the ancient Greeks sang, danced, performed dramas, and engaged in athletic competitions. For that reason, a god's place of 'worship' necessarily included a theatre and stadium. Thus, at Epidauros Menno found a wonderfully intact stadium from the 4th century BCE, with some original stone seating still in place. He also tested the acoustics of the famous theatre, still in use today. Menno sat in the top row of the theatre where he could observe the visitors and hear the amazing demonstration of acoustic perfection. Here Menno pondered the ancient story of Asklepios.

He was the son of Apollo and the mortal Koronis, who came from Thessaly. Koronis either abandoned her child, or was killed, leaving Asklepios to be brought up by Apollo, who gave him the gift of healing and the knowledge of the use of medicinal plants. He was tutored by the wise centaur of Mount Pelion, Cheiron (who also tutored Achilles). When Asklepios grew up he married Epione, and together they had several children: Machaon and Podaleirios – doctors who make an appearance in the *Iliad*, and daughters Iaso, Panacea and Hygeia. Descendants of Asklepios who continued the art of medicine and healing were known as Asklepiads, the most famous, whom we have met, was Hippocrates of Kos.

The myth tells us that Asklepios was killed by a thunderbolt of Zeus. Here we have another echo of the discord that brought suffering upon Prometheus. Asklepios was bringing gifts to humanity as the Titan had. Asklepios was blurring the line between the gods and humanity because his healing powers were formidable, and more importantly, because he could raise the dead. Asklepios was struck down for resurrecting Hippolytus, son of Theseus. Greek myths further record that Asklepios resurrected King Tyndareus and Glaucus son of Minos of Crete. Asklepios was deified after his death, and according to some accounts, he was himself resurrected by Zeus and given a place on Mount Olympus with the other gods.

After purification rites, patients who visited the Asklepeion at Epidauros would spend the night in the enkoimeterion (a place where patients slept) and where Asklepios would come to them in their dreams with remedies for their ailment. In many cases, patients were given a program of suggested exercise, diet, and surgery. Votive offerings left by the cured and thankful provide some idea of the range of illnesses, from hearing loss to pregnancy complications.

Asklepios was widely depicted in art across the Greek and Roman worlds, at other healing sanctuaries at Messene, Tegea, Pergamon, and at Athens, where

Sophocles was a part of the effort to bring the god there, and where a few columns of the Asklepeion are yet visible on the south slope of the acropolis. All of these healing sanctuaries along with all pagan sites, including Epidauros, were closed by decree of Emperor Theodosius II in 426 CE.

Upon returning to Nauplion, Menno discovered a taverna on a quiet back street. It was named παλιό αρχοντικο´ and was known for its tasty roast rooster dish. It was somehow fitting because the last words of Socrates recalled the image of Asklepios. Socrates' friend Crito was sent to fetch a cock and sacrifice it to Asklepios. It was what one did when being healed. Only Socrates, at the moment of his death, would proclaim that he was being healed! As Menno sipped his retsina he wondered how Asklepios and healing in antiquity were best understood. Perhaps ancient Greek medicine was the brilliant beginning of a lengthy tradition of caring for the sick in the West.

By contrast, the healing ministry of the New Testament is rarely to be found in Hebrew scripture in the Old Testament. It appears in the New Testament, rather as a natural continuation of the deep-rooted Greek experience. Moreover, like Jesus of Nazareth, Asklepios' one parent is god as father, and his mother is a mortal being. Both Asklepios and Jesus were healers and have followers who continue the tradition. And rather significantly, both are resurrected and deified, albeit in different ways. Perhaps because of Simone Weil's influence, or the carafe of retsina, or both, it seemed to Menno that there were continuities between the two lives, so separated by hundreds of years. There was much to ponder on his walk back to his room.

Troezen

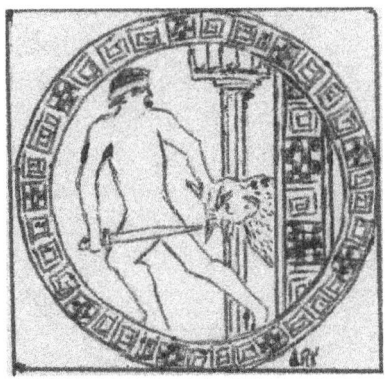

Theseus Slaying the Minotaur

The next morning Menno took a bus, by circuitous route, to Galatas, on the Saronic Gulf. Upon arriving at Galatas, Menno took a water taxi across the charming narrow strait to Poros. There he found an affordable room near a good taverna. The next morning he returned to Galatas where he began a long walk through olive, orange, and lemon groves with the ancient site of Troezen as his destination. His mission was to visit the site where Athenian women and children were evacuated, according to the plan of Themistocles, just prior to the invasion of the Persians in 480 BCE, and shortly before the calamitous defeat of the Persians by the Greeks at the Battle of Salamis. Troezen was also the site of the alleged birthplace of Athens' hero Theseus. It was in this vicinity as well, along the coast of the Saronic Gulf, where the death of

Hippolytus, son of Theseus, took place. Subsequently he would be resurrected by Asklepios, at the behest of Artemis whom Hippolytus worshipped.

Theseus was perhaps the most notable of the heroes of ancient Athens.[14] It is thought that his cult was established by the early eighth century BCE. After more than three hours of a delightful hike, Menno arrived at the sprawling abandoned archaeological site. Menno sat down with his lunch amidst wildflowers near the foundation of the Temple of Hippolytus, and there he recalled the richly embroidered past of Theseus. The hero was born to King Aegeus of Athens, or to the god Poseidon, and Aethra, daughter of Pittheus, King of Troezen, known throughout the Greek world for his wisdom. After sleeping with Aethra at Pittheus' invitation, Aegeus left instructions that if a son were born, he was to bring tokens to Athens — a sword and pair of sandals, which were left under a very large rock. A son was born and named Theseus. When Theseus reached an age that he could move the rock he was to present the sandals and sword to his father in Athens. Once he came of age, Theseus followed the instructions and made his way to Athens, choosing to travel the less safe route by land. The road was infested with murderers and bandits. Theseus proved himself capable of meeting each danger along the way. Each killer got what he deserved, in the tradition of 'an eye for an eye.'

Sinis, Phaia the wild sow, Cercyron and Procrustes each died in the fashion that they killed others. Sciron was wont to push travellers to their death off the cliff; and Theseus did to him the same near Megara. In short, Theseus rid the world of evildoers. He would later capture the destructive bull of Marathon – which he captured alive and dedicated to Apollo.

Shortly after Theseus arrived in Athens in the ninth year there was a time of famine and pestilence, and according to oracular instruction, Athens had to send seven young men and seven maidens to Crete. There, in a labyrinth, they were to perish as sacrifices to the part-man part-bull creature: the Minotaur. The tribute of unmarried sons of Athens was customarily determined by lot. However, out of pity for his fellow youths, Theseus volunteered to go in place of one of them and promised to slay the Minotaur and forever end the gruesome tribute. Theseus was allowed to go as part of the tribute and he met the man-beast in the labyrinth where he killed the Minotaur, and with the help of Minos' daughter Ariadne he found his way out of the labyrinth, and thus saved the others.

Upon the death of King Aegeus, Theseus became King of Athens. Over time, many great deeds were attributed to him, some quite unlikely in later times, given that he lived so much earlier. He committed many acts out of pity and kindness. Some alleged that he received Oedipus in Attica, blind and destitute, after he had unknowingly killed his father, and fathered children with his mother. He befriended Heracles after he had been driven mad and killed his own children. When King Creon refused rights of burial to the Argive side in the battle at Thebes, between the sons of Oedipus, Theseus is thought to have secured burial for the fallen, allegedly by means of a truce. In addition, he was to have helped Jason in the recovery of the Golden

Fleece, and Meleager in the hunt for the Calydonian Boar, and Heracles on another occasion in his pursuit of the Amazons along the coast of the Black Sea. In this campaign he abducted the Amazon, Antiope or Hippolyta.

By contrast, a well-known example of a kindness done by a friend was depicted in the pediment sculpture of the Temple of Zeus at Olympia. Theseus had gone to attend the wedding of Pirithous, King of the Lapiths in Thessaly. They had met in the past when Pirithous raided Theseus' cattle. The cattle thief was caught and quite readily forgiven, after which a long friendship ensued. At the wedding, the invited guests included centaurs, who after arriving to join in the celebration displayed poor judgment when they imbibed of alcohol instead of the sour milk provided for them. The centaurs proceeded to get out of hand and assaulted the Lapith women in attendance. On the pediment at Olympia, Apollo extended his arm over the fray, as though to ensure that all would be well. Indeed, Theseus came to the aid of Pirithous in driving the centaurs from the wedding and from his land.

There was also another side to the hero Theseus. This side is witnessed in his abduction of Antiope, his abandoning Ariadne on Naxos, after she had been his support while in Crete, his abduction of the very young girl, Helen, from Sparta, and the equally brazen attempt to carry off the goddess Persephone from the underworld. A life of heroic deeds for others, but also one of conquest for private gain, and one of thrilling escapades came to an end when Menestheus seized the throne at Athens in Theseus' absence. Theseus had sailed to Skyros, where he expected a warm welcome. Instead, he was killed by King Lycomedes when he was unexpectedly pushed off a cliff. His bones were recovered by Cimon in c. 475 BCE and laid to rest on the north slope of the acropolis of Athens, his home.

As Menno strolled about the small, excavated portion of ancient Troezen he concluded – in support of his hero cult – that there was much in the stories of Theseus that had to do with courage and taking great risks. He was one to assist his friends, but also to be open to forgiving the one stealing his cattle. More importantly, in his early years he volunteered to go to Crete, to face the Minotaur, in place of someone else. He was willing to risk his own life in order to save the other thirteen young people, and once and for always end the nine year sacrifice. Moreover, the place where Theseus' bones were laid to rest became a sanctuary—for runaway slaves, and the poor and oppressed. If Plutarch can be trusted, who lived over five hundred years after the recovery of the bones with the help of Cimon, Theseus was kind to the poor and could be counted upon to come to the aid of the distressed.

As Menno departed the modern village of Troezen he came upon a workman at the edge of an excavated hole. He greeted him with 'κάλη μέρα' and was surprised to hear three voices return the greeting; as there were apparently two courteous men working in the hole, unseen by Menno. This was not uncommon in Greece where its language also offered so many choices by which to greet the stranger: Γιάσσας hello, για Χαρά joy to you, χαίρετε the same, εμπρός on the telephone, and καλό μίνα a greeting at the beginning of the month.

On his stroll through the charming landscape on his way back to Galatas, Menno remembered that Troezen had been a member of an Amphictyonic League that was centred on Kalaureia, adjacent to Poros. This was an association of states enjoined in support of temples or sacred places like the Temple of Poseidon at Kalaureia. The associations looked after religious festivals and games, and also acted as alliances for the security of its members. Because of this association, it is likely that Kalaureia had an earlier name, 'Ειρήνη', or Peace. This early amphictyony was founded in the first half of the seventh century BCE and included as members, not only Troezen and Kalaureia, but Athens, Aegina, Epidauros, Hermione, Prasiais, Nauplion and Orchomenos.

Poros

Prometheus

Menno took the next day on Poros to make the long trek to the sanctuary of Poseidon. There he sat down with a view of the Saronic Gulf and Aegina and read one of his favourite plays, *Prometheus Bound* by Aeschylus.[15] Centuries before, the poet Hesiod had recorded that Prometheus was fastened to rock on a mountain top in the Caucasus Range, somewhere between the Black and Caspian Seas. Menno concluded that a trip to that mountainous region was out of the question, particularly because a view of the Saronic Gulf was more appealing. Reading Aeschylus' play would suffice to transport him to the play's setting.

Prometheus was a Titan from the beginning of time, his name meaning forethought, or providence. According to Hesiod, Prometheus was an arbiter in a contest between the gods and humankind, to decide which portion of a sacrificed animal was to be given to the gods and which to man. The arbiter determined that man would get the good meat. This may have been the beginning of a falling out between Zeus and Prometheus, but the story is larger. Not only did the figure of Prometheus bring fire, as it happens in the stem of the Giant Fennel plant, but he gave man as well the knowledge of construction of dwellings, work with baked bricks and wood, knowledge of the seasons, the stars in the firmament, work with metals, knowledge of the domestication of the horse, navigation on the seas by sail, and knowledge of letters and writing, numbers, medicine, and the ritual of sacrificing. Moreover, humans had been confused and lacked understanding. Perhaps Prometheus' greatest gift addressed this sorry state — he gave the gift of mind, understanding, and wisdom. All of these gifts were given by Prometheus to save humankind from annihilation by Zeus. In return, by being nailed to the mountainside, Prometheus is rendered powerless.

In his suffering, humiliation, and affliction, he is left totally abandoned – not unlike the Passion of Jesus. He paid the price for loving humankind, the price of justice, of balancing the scales. And justice was his legacy. Prometheus' mother is Themis, who is essentially justice itself, and is related to Gaia, the Earth, to Isis in Egyptian mythology, and Demeter, a mother of many faces.

Prometheus' chosen path is not that of might, but that of wisdom. He was alone among Titans to choose wisdom. Simone Weil sees Prometheus like Christ, as slain since the foundation of the world. For Menno there was indeed more than an inkling of resemblance. God is at the same time both benefactor and enduring servant, and the account points to the connection between suffering and love. As Weil is astute to notice, Zeus is not the protector of suppliants, he is Zeus Suppliant. The suppliant is at once worthy of pity, but also of respect.

The last lines of the tragedy read:

'O my mother and her holiness, O heaven
by whom the common light of all turns
do you see what wrongs I suffer?'
(ll. 1090-92)

The last word of the play is 'πασχω', or passion, recalling the line spoken by Ocean:

'There is no greater gain than to appear mad
because one is good',
To which Prometheus replies:
'That fault would seem rather to be mine.'
(ll. 385-86)

Prometheus Bound was the superb work of the playwright Aeschylus. He was born in Eleusis near to Athens in 525 BCE, while Pythagoras was yet alive. He died in Sicily in about 455. The years of his youth were ones of turbulence: the tyranny in Athens was coming to an end, to be replaced by Kleisthenes' introduction of the first early advances of democracy. The struggle against the attack of invading Persians followed, when it is thought Aeschylus took part in the Battle of Marathon in 490 BCE.

Aeschylus, the first of the great playwrights, for whom we have complete and extant plays, was a competitor in the Great Dionysia, in which he entered three tragedies and a satyr play. His first victory came in 484 BCE. Four years later, Aeschylus again participated in the military response to the Persians' invasion, this time at Artemesium and Salamis.

Another play of his – *The Persians* – was a reflection of his experience and won him a victory in 472 BCE. In Aeschylus' plays, his era is represented by the close integration of religious, social, and personal issues. For example, an individual's plight is more likely to be bound up with the community. Justice, δίκη, is central in the plays and is understood as divine justice. The nature of justice has often to do with human responses to success, which are often followed by a fall. The turning of fortune, or downfall, was understood as the inevitable product of pride or hubris. Zeus was the guardian of this universal fabric, ensuring that justice prevailed, even if it be delayed in some instances. That is the underlying circumstance in the Oresteia, the three plays — the Agamemnon, the Choephori, and the Eumenides. In these plays there is a unity — almost a single godhead of Olympian deities, who are in conflict with older deities, the Erinyes, or furies, that punish homicide, the killing of a mother or a father, and injury done to guests. They are the blind automatic force of vengeance. Agamemnon, King of Mycenae, returns victorious from Troy. He is struck down by his wife Clytemnestra, who in turn is killed by her son Orestes in revenge for having killed his father.

In this world, a king, husband, or father cannot be killed with impunity, not if an ordered society is sought, in place of anarchy and despotism. In the end all the subtleties of strife in the Eumenides find resolution; there occurs a final conciliation and combining of opposites. The goddess Athena brings to the court scene a presence of wisdom, tolerance and balanced judgment. Orestes is acquitted by reason and mercy as much as by votes in the court of the Areopagus. Endless repetition of retribution and vengeance has been supplanted by another way that is paramount to forgiveness and reconciliation. Zeus himself has prevailed without the use of thunderbolts, but through his daughter Athena's gift of persuasion.

On the way back to his room, Menno made a small detour to visit the stately, mauve Villa Galini, where Nobel Laureate George Seferis wrote and hosted friends that included Lawrence Durrell, Henry Miller and George Katsimbalis.

Milos

Aphrodite

The next morning Menno boarded a slow ferry bound for Aegina and Pireaus, where he then transferred to another ferry to Siphnos and Milos, his destination. Menno had lots of time to reread parts of Thucydides' extraordinary work, *The History of the Peloponnesian War*. Midway through the war, Athens may still have been the 'school of Hellas,' but it was not the same school it once was. In his funeral oration, as recorded by Thucydides, Pericles boasts that vengeance upon their enemies motivated Athenians, more than any personal blessings or gain.

Earlier when Menno had left Lesbos and the company of women, Anastasia had mentioned that she would be spending a few weeks on the Island of Kimolos assisting her grandparents. When she learned that Menno was to visit Milos, she invited him to stop by. Because Milos was dear to her heart, she suggested that they could also meet there. Menno accepted the offer and met her in the harbour when he arrived.

Menno made his way to the ancient acropolis of Milos, with the help of Anastasia, where once the exquisite sculpture, the Venus de Milo, was discovered, but also where in about 416 BCE the exchange between the envoys of Athens and the commissioners of Milos took place. Here Menno reread the Melian dialogue in Thucydides' *History*.[16] It was the sixteenth year of the war. The struggle for hegemony between Sparta and Athens was felt acutely by the smaller 'independent' states. Milos, though a colony of Sparta, had remained neutral in the war. With each year of war, more and more of these smaller states were forced to take sides, including Milos. To encourage the right outcome, the delegation from Athens was accompanied by a force of 1500 heavy infantry and 38 ships. They had come to 'negotiate' the island's surrender. If Milos became a part of the Athenian Empire their people and land would escape harm.

The Melians argued that they had a right to remain neutral, and that no nation had the right to attack without provocation. For Athens, there would be no talk of rights. At this time in their history, Athens had become the antithesis of so much of the 'wisdom' of archaic Greece. Brute force was pushing aside the practice of mercy and the demonstration of reason. It mattered not that Milos had remained neutral, but only that Athens had overthrown the Persians. Everyone knew that what was right was only applicable to equals in power. The strong do as they wish, and the weak states suffer. While this was the Athenian expression of realpolitik, the Melians appealed to the laws of nations and their common protection, which fell on deaf ears.

The Athenians saw neutrality and friendship as signs of weakness to their 'allies.' Counter to all that the School of Hellas had stood for in the past, the Athenians argued:

> 'Of the gods we believe, and of man we know that by necessary
> law of their nature they rule wherever they can…and as far as
> the gods are concerned we have no fear…'

The Athenians accused the Melians of blindness of judgment should they not surrender. Then the Melians remind the Athenians that by ignoring what is right and fair, the fall of the Athenians one day would be followed by the greatest vengeance. In the end, the Melians are to submit in order to avoid suffering, for they would not succeed in baffling the security of Athens, masters of the sea. The Melians maintained that any neutral states should wonder when their turn was coming, when they would be attacked and forced into the Empire. There is nothing here about right and honour and justice, the Athenians proclaimed, but only self-preservation before the threat of attack by a stranger. In fact, the true colours of hope are seen only after ruin, as well as the true colours of prophecies, oracles and other inventions; it is only then seen that man has been deluded. In this new order, justice and honour are accompanied by danger, while expediency ensures security. Besides, it is not dishonourable to give in to the greatest city-state in all of Hellas.

In the end, the Melians did not submit to brute force but instead invited the Athenians to be friends to them, and to be foes to neither Athens nor Sparta. Athens chose to put Milos under siege. The next winter the Athenians killed all the adult men in Milos and sold the women and children into slavery, and then sent five hundred colonists to inhabit the island themselves. In the dialogue, Thucydides revealed the transformation of Athens from the 'school of Hellas' to a tyranny.

When he had finished reading, Anastasia noted that the look on Menno's face was one of discomfiture. Had Thucydides rekindled a doubt about his whole pilgrimage and the parallels he saw between Mennonites and the Greeks? She reminded him that much had changed after Athens, with the help of allies, defeated the Persians. The city-state of Solon and Aeschylus was not like the city-state of Pericles, and it was not the exemplary city-state that children are taught about in school. Athens slowly became an imperial power, exacting increasing tributes from allies year to year. Anastasia added that – like today – alliances and resources were tied to strategic considerations.

Importantly, Anastasia felt that Menno should not lose sight of the separation of the conduct and views of political leaders from those of poets and playwrights (in this case, those of Thucydides). Had the focus of his pilgrimage not been the voices of those who reflect on the events in their lives? Like the *History* of

Thucydides? And for that reason, she was happy that Menno's pilgrimage included the historian.

Anastasia knew that Menno had left Lesbos after they met with plans to sail to Chios where he would have another look at the *Iliad*. Menno still had not said anything but was listening. Anastasia continued and was quite adamant about what was often missed in the reading of the poem. She said that Menno should not overlook the three voices with which Homer ends his epic poem: Hecuba and Andromache on the legacy of war—for women. And Helen who would always remember Hector with fondness, as he always had a kind word for her. Not so many academics, she thought, give attention to the voices of women in the poem.

After leaving the ancient acropolis, Anastasia insisted on giving Menno a tour of the island, a fantasy for lovers of geology. She brought him to the site where obsidian was mined and brought to the Peloponnese around ten thousand years ago. Through Anastasia's eyes and generosity Menno learned that the island had much to commend itself, even beyond the story in Thucydides. When they parted ways, Menno told Anastasia when he would be back in Athens and enquired if it might work that they see each other again; but not before thanking her for the support and understanding.

Eleusis

Demeter, Triptolemos and Kore
National Archaeological Museum

After returning to Pireaus, Menno's next stop was Eleusis, a site that to this day is surrounded by mystery. He contacted an academic colleague who drove him to the site – a half hour drive through heavy traffic in Athens. They found it in the midst of oil refineries and heavy industry, home to cults possibly dating back to Mycenaean times, and the setting of the salient and enduring myth known to most Greeks in antiquity.

Demeter was central to the myth. She was goddess of the earth, of agricultural fertility, of both plants and animals. One day, her daughter, Persephone (or Kore), disappeared while gathering wildflowers. She was abducted by the god Hades. He promptly carried her off to the underworld, where she was forced to become his wife. In a state of profound mourning, Demeter searched for her daughter, but to no avail. In her inconsolable state the world of plants and animals was no longer fertile and the entire earth no longer productive. A long winter set in.

In her search, Demeter was welcomed at Eleusis and it was there that she was told where her daughter was being kept. To placate both Demeter and his brother Hades, Zeus offered a solution: Persephone would spend two thirds of the year above ground with her mother; the other third, or the winter months, with Hades in the underworld. With this arrangement, fertility returned to the earth and the cycle of seasons resumed. To reward her kind hosts in Eleusis, Demeter gave them the knowledge of agriculture which Triptolemus was to pass along to others. The second gift was the Mysteries, the sacred knowledge to be experienced at Eleusis.

The Eleusinian Mysteries became a focus of the religious calendar of Athens. In the sixth century BCE, through efforts made during Pisistratus' time the Mysteries grew in repute as a pan-hellenic pilgrimage site. With the exception of people stained by blood guilt, the Mysteries were open to all adults, women and men, free or slave. Most Athenians would have been initiated after completing the required rituals. Every autumn Athens celebrated the week-long Great Eleusinian Festival. After performing sacrifices and purification rites, the celebrants walked to Eleusis along the Sacred Way, where festivities including initiation ensued. What the Mysteries bestowed was not to be revealed, but it was thought that initiates were shown the way to a happier life and death, as good things awaited them. According to Plutarch, all of this occurred in the midst of a marvelous light.

The Mysteries were celebrated at Eleusis for a period of about a thousand years. Olympian religion had various strands, including what Aeschylus wrote about in his plays — particularly the immutable laws of justice that were universal in scope. At Eleusis, religion took on a greater personal dimension, different from the salvation of humanity in the story of Prometheus. Life here on earth was transformed, but also the life hereafter!

The Eleusis archaeological site is a place of serenity in the midst of the darker manifestations of modernity. Fortification walls from the archaic period surround the site. A cave is prominent where Persephone was to have returned to her mother. The premier structure was the Telesterion, an enormous pillared and roofed hall that was enlarged over the years. It provided stepped seating along the inside walls, a palace or 'ανακτορον,' in the centre. The revelation to initiates was thought to have taken place here and was likely connected to the story of Persephone's return.

Menno was taken by the underlying meaning of the Mysteries. It was tempting to interpret the myth of Demeter and Persephone as one of rebirth and the promise of eternal life. The earth would blossom again in the spring through endless seasonal cycles that suggested the same for the destiny of humanity. And that a marvellous light materialized was suggestive of the Light that entered the world at Easter in Menno's tradition, as it happens at springtime as well. In the sixteenth century Anabaptist view, Easter also brought new visions of the beginning and end of human life, and of the offer to believers of rebirth, resurrection, and eternal life. In sum, for both the Ancient Greek Mysteries and the Easter passion, a great gift was given to humanity in the presence of Light (είμαι το φως του κόσμου, 'I am the Light of the world').

Before Menno left Eleusis, he stopped by the museum to see the sculpture in its collection, which did not disappoint. Menno observed the very early classical figure of the 'fleeing maiden,' a Hellenistic work of Persephone, and the lovely sculpture of Demeter, from circa 420 BCE, by the Parian sculptor Agorakritos, or that of his workshop. And there was also the bust of Athena emerging from a lotus flower — a reminder of the enduring shadow cast by the mysteries of Egypt.

Athens
Theatre of Dionysos, Ancient Agora, and Acropolis

Menno was back in Athens by evening, in time to enjoy an almost home-cooked dinner at κυρία Ζωή's hidden taverna on Mount Lykavettos, above Kolonaki. The ambiance of the taverna was a candle-lit semi-darkness, but the 'ζουζουκάκια' were brilliant. After a restful night in the neighbourhood, Menno walked past the Parliament Buildings and Syntagma Square to the Areopagus. Here Paul had preached to the Athenians in c. 51 CE, and it was where the seat of decision making was located in Solon's day. Solon was one of the seven sages, one who left his mark in Athens.[17] He was born in c. 630 BCE, a time of considerable turmoil. His leadership in the city-state was key to his legacy as lawgiver and sage.

Firstly, Solon appealed to his fellow Athenians through his poetry, and he helped them regain their honour by winning from Megara the strategic Island of Salamis. Second, the wealthy aristocrats, the eupatridae who owned the best land, made most decisions for all. In doing so, the poorer farmers were driven into serfdom, servitude, and slavery. Middle stratum farmers, merchants and craftsmen were excluded from participation in political life. Without intervention, events would inevitably unfold in favour of the loss of social cohesion, of revolt and tyranny.

In the years after c. 590 BCE, he became archon and lawgiver. Solon redeemed the forfeited land and freed those who had been enslaved by debt in a way that bears some similarities to the Jewish Golden Jubilee. In his poetry, the decree was described as 'a shaking off of burdens.' That included bringing back to Athens those sold into slavery and those who fled under constraints of debt. From this time forward a person could no longer be security for a loan.

Solon also ensured that produce other than olive oil could not be exported in order to guarantee sufficient quantities of grain for Athens' citizens. Measures were passed to support alternative occupations in the trades and professions. He had Athenian coins minted which facilitated trade and exports, particularly in olive oil and pottery. To the same end, new weights and measures were introduced, and the outcome of his reforms was a decrease in poverty.

Political reform took the form of replacing the eupatridae with wealthy citizens who were divided into four groups, based on a census of income which was measured primarily in grain, oil, and wine. Birth in a certain class was no longer a factor in determining participation in the affairs of the city-state. The general assembly – the ecclesia, to which all citizens were welcome – would come to pass laws, elect officials, and hear appeals in the courts. A Council of Four Hundred, with yearly rotation, was to prepare legislation for the Assembly. While these reforms paved the way to future democracy, many of the most important positions would still be held by the old aristocracy. In short, there was a lawgiver who brought order and stability to a state, and who sought adjustments in times of unforeseen change (precluding revolution), and one who could direct affairs to ensure fairness and justice for most citizens, such a lawgiver would appear to be very much the sage. Solon's esteem was only enhanced by his refusal to extend his political role. It was easy to accept the power and authority of a tyrant, he claimed, but much more difficult to give it up.

Solon's fame rests on his political and social reforms but he was also a merchant, a traveller, and a poet. In his poetry (such as the *Prayer to the Muses*) he proposes that riches unjustly won bring retribution, wealth won by violence is followed by ruin (sometimes soon thereafter, at other times to those born long after). For Solon it is best to restrain our greed and apportion orderly shares for all. Good government, in his *Political Verses*, displays order, puts shackles on those who break the law, levels rough places, stops greed and glut, and robs the force from violence; and good government straightens crooked judgments of courts, puts an end to strife, and 'stills the ill of wearisome Hate, and under her influence all life among humankind is harmonious and does well.' (*Greek Lyrics*, 21)

Menno left the Areopagus, overlooking the Agora and the marketplace, and spent the remainder of the day walking to several ancient sites including Plato's Academy, the ancient Kerameikos Cemetery, and what remains of the gigantic Temple of Zeus begun by Pisistratus in the sixth century BCE. Afterwards he visited the many building projects of the Emperor Hadrian, including the Gate near the Temple of Zeus and his Theatre on the south slope of the Acropolis.

Theatre of Dionysos, Acropolis, Athens

The next morning Menno entered the Acropolis Archaeological Site with the purpose of sitting in the famed theatre on the south slope of the Acropolis, the Theatre of Dionysos. For Menno, the theatre was sacred for the tragedies of Aeschylus, Sophocles and Euripides. On this day he wished to summon the spirit of Euripides, specifically *The Trojan Women*.[18]

Euripides was the youngest of the playwrights, and he was born c. 484 BCE and died in 406 in Macedonia or Salamis. His mother may have been a 'mere' greengrocer – a fact that the comic playwright Aristophanes poked fun at. Euripides' only public role was thought to be a diplomatic mission to Syracuse in Sicily. While still in his twenties he competed in his first dramatic contest. The ancients knew of over ninety plays he had written. He was not always well received, but he won victories for his plays at four festivals, was on many occasions chosen as laureate of the year and was given much attention by the critic and comic playwright Aristophanes.

Euripides' way of using the common myths and legends of the ancient Greeks was quite different than the conservative Aeschylus, his elder. For Euripides, the myths were approached with less reverence, with a rationalizing frame of mind, and with considerable scepticism. In keeping with his vantage on life, his characters were not larger than life heroes, but men and women of the marketplace who revealed current ideas and feelings. The plays exhibit ideas of social interest. His characters have tragic flaws and passions so that their suffering is of their own individual making — so unlike the characters in the tragedies of Aeschylus and Sophocles. Euripides' voice best reflected the shift in understanding of his fellow citizens, and anticipated that of the Hellenistic period, a time when realism and sensation held greater appeal. The playwright won the greatest popularity during this time, perhaps accounting for the survival of eighteen of his plays.

Euripides' play, *The Trojan Women*, was situated between the slaughter of male adults at the neutral Island of Milos, its forced entry into the Athenian Confederacy, and the disastrous launch – yet to occur – of the unprovoked expedition to conquer Sicily. The playwright takes his audience back to the salient war in the Greek consciousness, the Trojan War. The action in the play takes place between the fall of Troy—the Trojan warriors have been vanquished—and the departure of the Greeks. Understandably, *The Trojan Women* has been interpreted as an anti-war play, and one that members of Menno's Anabaptist Mennonite heritage may even have been familiar with.

Menno chose to sit right in front of the orchestra, which was a few rows above the area originally intended for dignitaries. He had Richmond Lattimore's translation of the play which he read over a period of two hours. Poseidon begins with a lament that the Trojans' sacred groves are desolate and the gods' thrones and temples are spotted in blood. At the outset of the play, the Trojan women are not yet assigned as slaves to specific masters. Because of the sacrilege shown the temples and tombs, Poseidon and Athena – who were on opposing sides in the war – agree to make the Greeks' homecoming a thing of sorrow. Their turn for suffering will come.

Hecuba, Queen of Troy, states that the fatal bride Helen has destroyed her city and has killed her husband Priam and her fifty sons. Her grey future will be forced labour in a foreign land. Talthybius, the messenger of the Achaeans to the Trojans, then brings the news of each woman's destiny and her new master. Euripides' depiction of the messenger is almost one of a friend, especially in his uncharacteristic tenderness. He is unable to bring himself to inform Hecuba that her youngest daughter, Polyxena, was sacrificed at Achilles' tomb, and is no longer alive. He can only tell her that she feels no pain.

Cassandra appears next. In the past she spurned the advances of Apollo and was punished with the gift of alone seeing the future, with no one believing or seeing what she sees. She was the daughter of Hecuba and King Priam, and was considered to be insane – a part of her punishment by Apollo. Such is her crazed state as she enters the stage, wishing to celebrate her new marriage-bed in Argos, next to her new master, King Agamemnon. Cassandra plays a part in developing a significant theme in Euripides' play: that the conqueror too will suffer along with the vanquished. That is the nature of war.

We have already learned that the return voyage over the sea by the Achaeans will be met with thunderbolts and storms, with drownings, and with vessels pushed off course, delaying their homecoming by years. To this Cassandra adds that Agamemnon will gain a new wife more fatal than Helen ever was. Agamemnon will die and bring untold suffering to his house, and Odysseus will face the terror of the Cyclops and Circe and struggle another ten years to get back to Ithaca.

One by one, the Trojan women are dragged off by new masters, to be taken to another land where they will bear the sons of Greek men. They leave behind their slaughtered brothers and husbands, slain next to the altars that were to protect them. Pain lies heaped over with pain, cries Hecuba.

Then Talthybius arrives with the news of the fate of Astyanax, decided by Odysseus. Earlier in the play, Odysseus has been described by Hecuba as vile, murderous, with a mouth full of lies and treachery, and the enemy of right! Astyanax is the son of Andromache and Hector. The small boy is his mother's last ray of hope, and this will now be shattered. Her son will be hurled from the tall battlements of Troy. The messenger advises Andromache to give in because she is powerless. She is then comforted by the promise that her child will receive a proper burial, covered with his father's shield and accompanied by a dirge of honour.

Andromache could not have imagined that the baby she had born was destined for butchery. In vain the labour pains, in vain nursing the swaddling child at his mother's breast. All of this is Greek barbarity, brought to Troy by (Helen) the daughter of vindictiveness, hate, blood, and death! The messenger is not capable of taking charge of Astyanax—out of pity—but hands him over to guards, to 'some other without pity.' Troy, once loved by the gods, is now forgotten.

Euripides then brings Helen on stage in defence of her part in the tragedy of the war. Paris had judged the fairest to be Aphrodite, over Hera and Athena. Helen maintains that her abductor had a goddess at Paris' side, when she was scooped from her home in Sparta. And besides, she had tried to escape many times to join the Achaeans during the war, but had been kept back. Hecuba and the chorus remain unmoved and call for Helen's death. Her husband, Menelaus, resists the advice. The chorus adds that in the end Zeus betrayed all to the Achaeans who would destroy all.

Talthybius attends to the body of Astyanax, washes the body himself, cleans his wounds and digs his grave. Hecuba wonders what made the Greeks so afraid as to savagely kill a child. She despises the fear that puts terror in the unreasoning mind. The boy lies with his head crushed, his small hands, like those of his father, lie broken at the wrists. Hecuba persists, declaring that the Greeks possess all their strength in their spears, not in their minds (ll. 1185-91):

'Now I, a homeless, childless, old
woman must bury your poor corpse,
which is so young....'

She adds,
'What shall the poet say,
what words will he inscribe upon your tomb?
Here lies a little child the Argives killed, because
they were afraid of him.'

Earlier in the play Hecuba has reflected on Zeus with a positive spirit, albeit the rationalizing approach of the playwright:

'O Power, who mounts the world,
wheel where the world rides
O mystery of man's knowing, whosoever you be
Zeus named, nature's necessity or mortal mind,'
And ends with a return to the necessary balance:
'I call upon you; for you walk the path none hears
yet bring all human action back to right at last.'
(ll. 884-88)

Hecuba ends in despair: the gods have meant nothing but to make life hard for her. In vain they had sacrificed to the gods. Indeed, even burying the dead with tokens of luxury makes little difference to the dead (an echo of Archilochus). Hecuba underlines the theme of doubt when she questions the worth of calling on the gods for help, as they did not hear before. And as the last women are taken away to slavery, Troy 'fades as smoke winged in the sky' (l. 1299). King Priam is left without a grave, forlorn and nameless, and we readers are to mourn for the ruined city and its people.

Between the euphoric years after the Greek defeat of the Persians at Salamis, and the prolonged agony of the Peloponnesian War, more than thirty years later, a major, if gradual, shift in outlook took place in Greek thought. The change was characterized by the desire to pursue rhetoric, by a disillusionment in past ideals, and a greater appeal of emotion and sentiment. There is a draw toward realism best embodied in the sculpture masterpieces of Skopas and Praxiteles. This shift was accompanied by increasing doubt and uncertainty in social and political life – a shift not unlike the one taking place in Menno's own time.

Simon the Cobbler's workshop
Agora Archaeological Site of Athens

Menno's next stop was in the agora, the marketplace, in the shadow of the Acropolis. There he wished to ponder the life of an ancient Greek who was larger than life, one still inextricably linked to persisting questions of our day because of his legacy. He was the passionate citizen of Athens, philosopher and martyr: Socrates.[19] He led his fellows in a new direction, toward horizons not before seen in Athens. Menno chose to take a seat in a cobbler's shop that, in Socrates' day, had belonged to Simon. This was one place Socrates visited, as recorded in the *Dialogues of Plato*. Archaeologists found at this site cobblers' nails and Simon's cup, only a small part of the amazing excavation conducted by the American School of Classical Studies in Athens.

Unlike the challenges faced by researchers studying our earlier sages, or the example of Pythagoras, a quite reliable picture of Socrates' life has been passed down to our time. Our sources include the extensive conversations found in the *Dialogues of Plato*, the Memorabilia, the Symposium, the Apologia and Oeconomicus of Xenophon, the comedic plays of Aristophanes, and references in Aristotle – who did not meet Socrates, but had the benefit of having studied for years at Plato's Academy.

Socrates, a native Athenian, was the son of Phaenarte and Sophroniscus, a stone mason or sculptor. He was born in 470-69 BCE, and likely followed his father's profession. He was married to Xanthippe with whom he had three sons. In his public life he received high praise for his courage, shown in three military campaigns, all during the Peloponnesian

War: the siege of Potidaea, the defeat of Athens at Delium in Boeotia in 424, and the Battle of Amphipolis two years later. He allegedly stood out for his bravery and for saving lives, like that of Alcibiades. In 406 Socrates supported the hearing of separate cases against generals charged with failing to rescue their men from wrecked ships at Arginusae. He also served his turn in the Council and earned the reputation of following his inner convictions, without regard to any political party. In this spirit he opposed the oligarchy of the Thirty, two years later.

Socrates was considered 'ugly' by his contemporaries, given his snub nose, thick lips, and protruding eyes. He was normally observed wearing the same worn coat, and barefoot. He consistently exhibited a hardiness and self control that enabled him to walk barefoot in the winter, as he did at Potidaea. Moreover, he would only drink wine to comply with social custom and to enhance good conversation. When called to do so, he would out-drink anyone, but he never became inebriated. Similarly, his appetite for sex as for food was controlled, and he also showed an indifference to material pleasures. At one time, upon entering the agora with his friend, he exclaimed: 'look at all the things (for sale) that I have no need of.' Socrates was very much an ascetic, in the Pythagorean manner.

Perhaps as important as anything in Socrates' approach to acquiring wisdom was his humanist leaning. He was not so much interested in how the world was put together, as so many of the earlier philosophers were. The natural philosophy of Thales and his followers was not the focus of Socrates' interest. Upon encountering a friend while Socrates was making his way to Athens, he explained that where people are – in cities – that is of true interest to him, and by contrast: 'trees and the open country have nothing to teach me' (Phaedrus, 230d).

In some ways, Socrates shared in the norms of his time as regards sex and love, for example. It was widely held that courtesans – for example in the relationship between Aspasia, Pericles, and Socrates – were for platonic pleasure, and concubines were for physical gratification, and wives for the procreation of lawful offspring. A wrong type of love was physical gratification, one that faded along with good looks and youth. The right type was the love of another's spirit, rather than body alone, which thereby can nurture an ennobling friendship. One might conclude from this that Socrates had his sexual passions under control and that his relationships brought with them the gift of seeing with new eyes. In the *Symposium*, Socrates argues that *eros* (love) helps to recall the knowledge of beauty without 'erotic' aspiration, and further contributes to an understanding of spiritual truth.

Throughout Socrates' life, he had experiences with his 'daimonion,' a divine sign that revealed itself to him as an inner voice. This voice directed Socrates not to do certain things. He believed in a direct relationship between himself and the divine. In keeping with this understanding, when Chaerephon went to the Delphic Oracle and asked if there was anyone wiser than Socrates, the Oracle pronounced that there was no one! Socrates responded: 'if that be so it must mean that the wise know their own shortcomings, know that they do not know.'

Further in keeping with his relationship to the divine, Socrates left behind his earlier enthusiasm for natural science – as already mentioned – because it neglected human problems and final causes. It was better, he urged his younger friends, to care for their souls. In Socrates' mission he embraced the unity exemplified in the life of Pythagoras a century earlier, especially his search for a true understanding of the world and the self. Similarly, Socrates was adamant in turning his back on the pursuit of money, honour, and reputation, in favour of taking thought for wisdom, truth, and psyche, or the soul. This effort may have been religious, but it was also largely philosophical and intellectual. Psyche in Socrates' thought may be akin to the divine, and also referring to something capable of an afterlife, as in Pythagoras' teaching, or it may be associated with the power of thought and mind, or something within us, as a microcosm of the universe that is capable of attaining wisdom and truth.

For him, self-knowledge alone could lead to the good life, as in the sages' maxim 'γνῶθι σαυτόν.' In the Alcibiades Dialogue of Plato, Socrates proposes that to truly know yourself, you must see that the soul resembles God and that you must look to God and wisdom. In the Memorabilia of Xenophon, Socrates states: 'Just consider that your own mind within you controls your body as it will. So you must believe that the wisdom in the whole universe disposes all things according to its pleasure' (Mem. I. 4-17). More than anything else that is human, the soul partakes of the divine. A supreme God of the universe cares for human beings and loves them, and at the same time is the supreme Mind who orders the cosmos (Apology 41d, cf. 1 John 4).

To perfect our souls requires knowledge of virtues and how to obtain them. When we act wrongly it is out of ignorance (not unlike the words of Jesus, 'Father forgive them for they know not what they do.'). Socrates was a teacher who taught through inquiry by asking questions, by pursuing definitions and seeking the essence of things, like the question 'what is friendship?' Interestingly, like Jesus of Nazareth and possibly Pythagoras, Socrates left no writings. Nonetheless, we are left a clear imprint of another sort, one that reveals the spirit of his inquiry. Socrates was clear that doing injustice was worse for oneself than being subjected to an injustice; or, in other words, it was better to suffer wrong than to do wrong (Gorgias, 469-522). He firmly rejected the contemporary and deeply held view that it was best to aid one's friends and harm one's enemies, that vengeance, returning wrong for wrong was the better way. His way was rather to make a friend of an enemy. To accomplish this he required an articulated understanding of the virtues; and these taken together were the same in essence as justice, wisdom, and self control.

At the age seventy, Socrates was brought on trial for his life, on charges of impiety, of not believing in the city's gods, and corrupting Athenian youth. In the Apology of Plato, Socrates points to his interest in justice. Unlike the sophists with whom he is confused, and unlike Evenus of Paros who takes a fee, Socrates does not accept recompense for his work.

Importantly, Socrates submitted to the judgment of the city-state in a spirit of obedience without regard for his own convictions. For Menno, Socrates' submission to the collective known as Athens was startlingly similar to the submission of the Anabaptists when they placed the views of the congregation (or *gemeinde*) before those of the individual. The priority was the community, the collective. In Socrates' defence he is concerned with right and wrong, not his own life or death. He greets his jurors with respect, and is grateful to them, (not unlike Jesus in Matthew 5:46), but in the end he must obey God, for the good of the city. Socrates is found to be guilty and is sentenced to death. His response is not to be angry with those who accused him, nor the jurors who convicted him, for they were mistaken and did not know what they were doing. Socrates says he has been obedient to his divine mission, to examine justice, goodness, and beauty, the greatest good (μέγιστος αγαθός), and to discuss virtue (αρετή), for the unexamined life is not worth living (Apology 38a). Before Socrates drinks the hemlock, he proclaims that he goes to die, and his friends remain behind to live, and which is the better is known alone to God. His last words are addressed to his friend Crito; he is to fetch a rooster and sacrifice it to Asklepios, the healer; and thereby the philosopher leaves a suggestion as to which he thought is the better.

Menno left the agora in silence, both saddened and uplifted. He wished to cherish a passage from Plato's *Symposium*:

'The most important is that Love neither causes nor submits to injustice, be it among the gods or among men. For when suffering happens to him he does not suffer by force, for force cannot reach Love...' (196b)

As Menno made his way to his room in the Plaka, via the promenade dedicated to Dionysius the Areopagite – Paul's first convert in Athens – he wondered about the work of artists, other than bards and poets and philosophers. The architects and sculptors also left their legacy throughout Greece. Different subjects were featured in the temples, as in the Panathenaic procession on the frieze of the Parthenon. Or, the birth of Athena depicted in the tympanum. Yet, in so many examples it seemed the depiction of struggle and conflict predominated. The Temple of Aphaia on the Island of Aegina was built at the end of the archaic period, or about 495 BCE. Here scenes of the Trojan War were sculpted in the pediments.

The eastern pediment of the Temple of Zeus at Olympia is later, from 470 BCE. It depicts the dramatic beginning of a chariot competition. The western pediment shows the violent conflict between Lapiths and Centaurs at the wedding of Pirithous where Theseus was in attendance. Elsewhere, in Athens, Poseidon and Athena vie for control of Athens. The eastern pediment of the Temple of Asklepios at Epidauros features the sack of Troy. The sculptor Timotheos here chose to sculpt the scene of Neoptolemus stabbing the aged King Priam. The frieze of the fifth century BCE Temple of Poseidon at

Sounion featured the battle with the centaurs. From the same period the Temple of Hephaistos in the agora of Athens shows the battle between Theseus and the Pallantides, and on the west end again the battle between the Lapiths and Centaurs. The metopes here catalogue the feats and labours of both Theseus and Heracles, his cousin.

~

Menno was left with too many questions. Were there lessons in the temple sculpture? Why were so many temples of the gods the chosen venue to remind Greeks of battle and strife? What was it about the Trojan War that incised its story in the Greek consciousness for centuries? Like Cheiron, centaurs were healers and mentors, but others forgot to drink their sour milk and assaulted the women at a wedding. Does the recurrent treatment of Pirithous' wedding point to two currents running through human beings; two very different choices? On the Trojan Plain a recurrent horror is the scene of a warrior's body being consumed by vultures and dogs. Is the Greek sentiment in this story that humanity is more than animal in nature, more as revealed in Patroclus' rebuke of Achilles, that he is the offspring of determinant forces?

The same temples were sacred spaces for the worship of a deity, but also sanctuaries. The sacred space – the *temenos* – was delineated by a wall. Demosthenes came to the Temple of Poseidon in Kalaureia to evade his assassins, but he could not die within the sanctuary. Mortals could not die within temple sanctuaries, nor could women give birth in the same confines. In other words, life could neither begin nor end there. We read that this was the case at the sanctuary for Asklepios in Epidaurus and Apollo's sanctuary at Delos.

At Olympia, as Menno learned, the temenos was off-limits to anyone bearing arms. The violation of Trojan Temples during the war with the Achaeans was sacrilege and led to the disasters that befell them thereafter. There was a sanctuary on the north slope of the Acropolis, in conjunction with the burial site of Theseus. This site was first a sanctuary after Cimon discovered the bones of Theseus in the north Aegean and returned them to Athens. Theseus was thought to be sympathetic to the plight of runaway slaves, of exiles and fugitives. Plutarch writes (Thes. 36-2) that Theseus' tomb is a place of refuge for slaves and all those wretches who fear people who are stronger since the hero Theseus was both their champion and supporter and responded in kindly fashion to the needs of the downtrodden. Such sanctuaries dotted the landscape of Hellas to offer some degree of protection and security, when custom and the law failed to do so.

Menno's pilgrimage to Greece certainly appeared adumbrated next to the celebrated traveller of the second century CE, Pausanias. He was born in Lydia and flourished during the reigns of the Emperors Hadrian, Antoninus Pius and Marcus Aurelius. His primary interest was the religion of the earlier centuries in Greece. While on Mount Helicon Pausanias was shown a sheet of lead with a passage of Hesiod's *Works and Days* inscribed thereon. There too he was shown statues of Hesiod, Arion and Orpheus. On the base of the statue of Zeus in Olympia Pausanias discovered the inscription: 'Pheidias the son of Charmides from Athens made me.' In Thebes Pausanias was still able to see the house of the poet Pindar.

So reliable was Pausanias in his first-hand accounts of his travels, that archaeologists could literally follow his description to a specific site. At Olympia (Eleia, Book V), Pausanias directed archaeologists to so many sites within the temenos, including Pheidias' workshop where he fashioned the famed statue of Zeus. There they found a cup with Pheidias' name inscribed on the bottom, and molds and sculptors' tools. In Pausanias' words:

> 'There are a lot of truly wonderful things you can see and hear in Greece, but there is a unique divinity of disposition about the mysteries at Eleusis and at the Games at Olympia.'

Parthenon, Acropolis, Athens

The next morning Menno decided to pay a visit to the Acropolis and the Temple of Athena, the renowned Parthenon. He spent the morning admiring the temple that was built between 447 and 432 BCE, with tributes collected by coercion from Athens' empire. The building program was to honour Athena, to glorify Athens, but there was also more. The Parthenon displayed no straight lines or perfect right angles. Instead, architects – chiefly Ictinos and Callicrates, under the supervision of Phidias – incorporated refinements that corrected optical illusions. To begin, the structure reveals proportions of length to width, of root-five to one. The golden ratio is employed in the façade, which is approximately 1.618. The temple was a masterpiece of advanced geometry. With Pythagoras we can see that the Greek mind saw mathematics as a means to understand the divine. There is no temple in Greece that better exemplifies this principle.

The refinements were numerous and called for incredible skill in their implementation. The stylobate, or top section of the foundation is six centimetres higher in the centre, both in the width and length of the building. This convexity is applied to other architectural members: the frieze, architrave, and cornice. The outer columns are closer together near the ends of the row. The sculpted metopes similarly are spaced closer to each other near the ends of the length of the temple. The corner columns are wider than the others. All columns taper upward and swell in the centre, called entasis. In addition, all columns tilt toward the centre and would meet somewhere in the sky if extended. Taken together, the refinements create the sense of straight lines and the impression of perfection.

There will always be a debate as to why the Greeks put in place this amazing assortment of refinements. Menno agreed with the classicists who believed that for the ancient Greeks there was a direct link between universal laws (as in mathematics) and the divine. To ancient Greeks, the act of incorporating these laws in the architecture of a building created a harmony, or a golden ratio.

This understanding may have endured for centuries but began to alter in the fourth century. In the fifth century BCE, sculptors like Phidias fashioned subjects that in their lightness almost hovered above the ground. They are in a space that is beyond pain and almost outside of time itself. The statues appear as though proportions are perfect, with a harmony that defines them. As the years passed, sculptors like Lysippos, Praxiteles, and Skopas fashioned stunning figures, but with a difference: they were softer and displayed emotion and pain. Perhaps a devotion to realism had set in. The memorable funeral stelae of Skopas, on display in the National Archaeological Museum, are exquisite works of art. They are exhibits of great sadness where the emotions are not controlled, but rather released.

While on the Acropolis, Menno looked down upon the exact sites where democracy was practiced in ancient Athens. In the early years, after the reforms of Kleisthenes – that is after 508 BCE – the assembly (εκκλεσία) met in the Agora, on the north side of the Acropolis. To the west, Menno could see the ridge where assembly gatherings took place at the Pnyx. After the beginning of the fifth century, the assembly held meetings in the Theatre of Dionysos, where the dramatic festivals also took place, on the south slope of the Acropolis. As well, Menno could look down on the theatre and the columns of the Asklepion west of the theatre.

Democracy may have begun earlier and existed elsewhere than Athens, but here is likely the site of its earliest expression in Europe. The early attributes of democracy changed over time; however, there were several that were of particular interest to Menno. These attributes seemed to echo the ideas of earlier times, those of Pythagoras and the sages and later poets. For balance and harmony, Kleisthenes had created new demes which mixed the classes, trades, and regions — so that no one group could rule over the others. Similarly, the use of the lot assured that executive positions could not be independent of the ekklesia. Importantly, there was a fundamental principle of equality at play; perhaps Pythagoras' view that equality was friendship was yet alive and well. 'Ἰσονομία' was a crucial buttress of democracy: it ensured equality of political rights and potential to exercise power (every citizen held an office at least once in twenty years). It underlined a method of balancing opposites and binding together in harmony the body of citizens. Moreover, a law, or 'νόμος', was a statute necessarily arrived at by common agreement, and was equally binding on both the ruler and the ruled.

In ancient Greece, artists were seen as educators; one gained knowledge and understanding by attending plays. The satyric plays were often critical of political figures in the city-state. In addition, the theatre admission was subsidized to ensure that all who wished could attend. This was necessary because the democracy of Athens was not representative, but participatory. If the majority of citizens – conspicuously restricted to male adults aged eighteen and older, excluding women, foreign residents, and slaves – were to participate and make wise decisions, education would need to play an essential role. It was important to be a part of the affairs of your city-state. This was evidenced by the name given one who was private in motivation, not taking time for public life — 'ιδιότης' or our word idiot. It was also underlined by the seriousness of holding office. 'Ευθυνη' was the name given to the significant institution of the end of term audit, or reckoning. All executive positions, either elected and appointed, or determined by lot, were subject to an evaluation at the end of the one year term.

For Menno, democracy itself could not have been imagined, let alone instituted, if egalitarianism and equality, if balance and harmony in preference to coercion, were not held in high regard. These ideas had been with Greek society, in fragmentary form, since the seven sages and Pythagoras. Menno lamented that some of the earlier tenets of ancient Greek democracy had been lost through time. He believed that it may have been inevitable, as suggested by Heraclitus in the early fifth century BCE when he claimed that: 'you cannot step into the same river twice.' However, every renaissance has been an attempt to do just that by returning to an earlier time through the study of original works of art, literature, governance and more. Menno believed that like words whose meanings evolved through time, institutions of governance would drift away from their roots.

He also noted that what we refer to as religions are not exempt from these forces of change. In his studies, Menno became more certain that the divide between the pagan world and early Christianity in the first century was more porous than commonly understood. Athena's temples were often built upon and dedicated to the Virgin Mary, as were temples of Asklepios, which became churches dedicated to the healing Saints Cosmas and Damian.

The genius of Menno's heritage – the Anabaptist tradition and Mennonite faith – was to recognize that a lengthy tradition of faith will lead in directions not foreseen at the outset. The unfolding of tradition will sometimes lead to outcomes that contradict its original and foundational teachings. In response to this, the Anabaptists in sixteenth century Switzerland and the Netherlands, and soon thereafter in German speaking territories, sought to return to the example of the early church. In doing so, several tenets of their faith sharply contrasted with those of the late medieval Church.

The Anabaptists believed that membership in a community of believers should only be one of free will, and something possible only for adults. There should be no coercion in matters of faith, they thought. Anabaptists held the view that converts in the early church were adults and therefore infants were not supposed to be baptized. Rather, the Anabaptists baptized their adult members for the first time (if they had not been baptized as infants) and baptized their followers again (if had been baptized as infants, when they had no choice in the matter). Hence the label given those of this view was 're-baptists,' or 'Anabaptists.'

Very early in the movement, when Conrad Grebel resisted the course taken by his mentor and Zurich reformer Ulrich Zwingli, he decided not to submit to the city council. At first, the separation of church and state was implied, but later it became an explicit value. As well, their refusal to take the oath followed Jesus' exhortation to speak the truth at all times in a way that did not require the additional assurance of oaths, and this position was also reflected in the Anabaptist resistance to pledging allegiance to the state.

From the beginning, in the Anabaptist branch of the Radical Reformation, followers were taught not to conform to the ways of the world. This aspect of their faith was based on New Testament teachings and further cemented by centuries of persecution, resulting in thousands of martyrs recorded in books like *The Martyrs' Mirror*. The Anabaptists needed to remain out of view, if not hidden, to survive. Both asceticism and the free sharing of goods – sometimes in the form of holding possessions in common (*omni sunt communia*) – were practiced by Anabaptist groups.

A salient reason that the established churches – both Catholic and Reformed – were driven to root-out the heretics was that they did not recognize the hierarchy within their churches. For the Anabaptists, authority rested upon the Scriptures and their communal form of interpretation in which each member had a voice. Anabaptists referred to this as 'the priesthood of all believers' (cf. 1 Corinthians 4:1). In most cases, Anabaptist leaders were chosen by their congregation, but there were also charismatic figures who gathered followers around themselves. Without an explicit hierarchy, the Anabaptists began churches through the free decision of individuals, allowing for differences among them and also greater autonomy.

Within a few decades of the first gatherings of Anabaptists they defined their position on not doing harm to others. In time, support for non-resistance became the norm for most Anabaptists. Force was never supposed to be used, even for self defence when under attack. Anabaptists were enjoined to turn the other cheek. They aspired to love their neighbour, which meant their enemies as well. They could not comply with military service in good conscience because killing another person was forbidden. This position was not only a further cause for persecution, but a reason why people of Menno's heritage migrated from one place in Europe to another, and eventually moved to new continents — all in order to escape conscription, participation in war, and persecution.

Menno's pilgrimage to Athens and beyond in Greece was an attempt to examine the thinking of bards, poets, sages, and philosophers, and in particular voices from antiquity who foreshadowed important tenets of Anabaptism. It was not evident to Menno how this came to be. He was not one to identify direct lines of causality and connectivity, but at the same time he favored Simone Weil's commitment to the idea that there is a clear continuum between ancient Greece and the Gospels. He also felt that there were patterns evident in history, and agreed with Thucydides, that because of human nature, history would at some point in time, and in much the same way, be repeated.

Here, near the end of his pilgrimage, Menno still remained in awe of the coincidences between a select number of voices of ancient Greece and voices from his own Anabaptist heritage. The importance of belonging, whether as a citizen of a city-state or a member of a fellowship, was shared between these two groups, so separated in space and time. The compelling ideas of egalitarianism – without which the birth of democracy may not have been witnessed in Athens, and the absence of hierarchy in Menno's faith – were also held in common across lines of difference. The maxims of several of the sages that persuasion was better than force and coercion, were clearly also found in Anabaptist thought, especially in the works of those who faced coercion from the established churches.

The centrepiece of agreement is likely found in the presence of voices of dissent within both cultures. These voices held that war was the bane of humanity, as reiterated in the *Iliad*. In all cases, war ended with both victor and vanquished being defeated. Suffering and the destruction of the beauty of life was the price of war. In the complex origins of Anabaptism, there were individuals who made room for violence. Yet, by about 1540, a form of pacifism became a defining part of the movement's interpretation of the New Testament. By the middle of the sixteenth century, many Anabaptists proclaimed their unique way of non-resistance. The killing of another human being was not only prohibited by the gospels, it was also simply wrong. While the poet Archilochus may have pointed the way to this conclusion, he was not a pacifist. Nor were the sages who counselled against the use of force where persuasion was the better course. However, Pythagoras' understanding of harmony, his forbidding of the sacrifice or harm to animals, and his aversion to killing his fellow person, were very much in the spirit of the teachings of Jesus of Nazareth, and the teachings followed by Anabaptists. And for Menno, the figure of Pittakos was very much of the same understanding, when he advised that people should not do to others what they would not want done to them.

Religions of various stripes seemed to become more complex as time passed, being both blessed and burdened with accretions of ritual, detailed articles of a dogmatic nature, and lists of things to be done and things not to be done. Christianity was no exception. Menno came to believe that much about religion was indeed tied to ritual, and while some accretions were extraneous, in their origins an embryonic form is revealed. When pressed by the Pharisees about what laws were to be followed, Jesus professed that people should love their neighbours as they love themselves, and as they love God with heart, strength, and mind. That was the embryo of Christianity which Anabaptists tried to translate into daily living. This meant that one should love the enemy as one would love a neighbour. In word, this meant not speaking ill of your enemy, as the sages counselled. In deed, it meant coming to the aid of the dispossessed and those in need. It meant practicing mutual aid to ensure equality and an active life of peacemaking, including the arbitration of disputes to prevent violence and suffering – a teaching and practice linking the early Sacred Truce of the Games and Pythagoras, to the members of Menno's heritage.

The alternative is portrayed in graphic detail in Homer's *Iliad*, and by others such as Euripides and his fellow playwrights. In his lectures, H. D. F. Kitto taught that the tragedies of Aeschylus, Sophocles, and Euripides were a form of religious literature. In their plays there was evidence of the desire to search for unity and order. The plays were about conflict and reconciliation, chaos and order, and always justice. Justice must assert itself: 'χρόνος δικάζει,' which is to say that time brings with it the fulfillment of justice. Moreover, things come to be as a part of a *logos*, or pattern that is the will of the gods. In their work, the gods are to be understood together, and represent the immanent laws and conditions of human existence. Wisdom meant knowing one's place in this ordered world, and knowing that an eternal rhythm pervades the cosmos and that human beings are part of this. For the Greek playwrights, the gods collectively prefigure a world order which is the context and background of our lives. Thus, the nature of religious thought in the ancient Greek context centred on the contemplation of the universe and its working order. Religious myths were a compass, a means of conveying thought and grappling with the realities of the present. The gods in these myths reveal that religion is coterminous with life itself and that the particular and universal aspects of the same action are fused together, connecting the microcosm and the macrocosm. This way of thinking and the Greek desire for understanding the world led to the particular expressions and voices heard at the various sites along the way of Menno's meanderings.

At the outset Menno was aware of the early church fathers' response to being introduced to such startling similarities between the views held by Socrates and Plato and those of the New Testament teachings of Jesus. They came up with the term *homo naturaliter Chrisitianus*, the naturally Christian person who was drawn to goodness and granted the grace to lead a moral life without the benefit of biblical revelation. In keeping with this understanding, and upon the completion of Menno's pilgrimage, he could imagine a group of people who lived millennia ago in ancient Greece holding hands – like the *ekecheiria* of participants in the Sacred Truce in the Olympic Games – with the Mennonites of his day.

Postscript

A farewell dinner had been arranged. Not for Menno, but for Virgil. Menno had made his decision. He would remain in Athens where he had accepted the job offer from the American college. Anastasia, who seemed pleased with Menno's decision, would join them for the farewell. The three would soon meet at a taverna frequented by Menno in his earlier student days – the Philippou Taverna on Xenokratous Street. The taverna had been there for decades, above Kolonaki Square.

Upon meeting, Virgil launched into an account of his adventures on Mount Athos, Anastasia spoke of being with her grandparents on the Island of Kimolos, and Menno recounted his day trip to Eleusis. As expected, they savoured a delectable feast with retsina from the barrel — the perfect complement. For some time, they discussed sites that should not be missed when visiting Greece, each suggesting destinations that reflected their interests.

Halfway through the evening, Anastasia introduced Menno and Virgil to the Alexandrian-Greek poet C. Cavafy. His poem 'Ithaka' was not about recommendations for *what* to see. It was about *how* to travel; how to allow the journey to act as a midwife for new birth; how to understand the unfamiliar. Anastasia had led small tour groups and shared that too many travellers could not leave their ego and all its accoutrements behind. They could not travel unnoticed as spirits. And thus, the many rewards of travel were withheld from them. Anastasia confessed that she interpreted Greek culture – the famous sites and people – from the distinct vantage point of being Greek, a woman of Greek Orthodox faith, and one belonging to a heritage of hardship and suffering, particularly following her parents and grandparents. Through her tours she had met people from abroad who helped her to see and understand her own culture differently. In a way, she thought, Menno was just such a person.

Menno then announced to Virgil that he was staying in Athens. He acknowledged that his family and church back home would not be pleased with his decision and would not understand his reasons for remaining in Greece. The rift would remain for him and his family. But he hoped they would find agreement one day. For Menno, the pilgrimage had reinforced his desire to continue studying. It had also softened the distinction between his Anabaptist Mennonite heritage and the salient Greek voices he found along the way.

Virgil had been mostly silent, listening and smiling.

'I have a confession to make. Over the years I met your stepfather on several occasions at church conferences. We even exchanged letters. Paeta knew I was planning to be in Greece at this time, exploring old haunts and seeing old MCC friends (at which point Menno finally caught on). He asked if I would not keep an eye on you and steer you in the right direction. You see, he passed along your approximate itinerary. That is, when we met along the way, it was not by accident.

'Yet, at the end of my stay I sense I have not carried out my mission. Perhaps my heart was not totally aligned with Paeta's objectives. I fear that you, Menno, have influenced me, more than I altered your views.

After giving it some thought, perhaps my experience with MCC on Crete could be more instructive than I had first thought. Could it be that to understand the unfamiliar – as Anastasia suggested – means walking in another's shoes, and rubbing shoulders with them in work? Through listening? Maybe a continuing dialogue between contemporary Mennonites and the ancient Greeks would not be such a bad idea.'

And so, the evening ended with Anastasia, Virgil, and Menno each sensing that the pilgrimage was not at an end, but truly just beginning.

About the Author

Ronald Tiessen was raised in a Mennonite family and fellowship outside Leamington, Ontario. His studies brought him to Conrad Grebel College, the University of Waterloo, the University of Windsor, and thereafter to Greece. After studying Ancient Greek history in Athens, he made his home on Pelee Island, the setting of his 2016 novel *The Pele' Harbour for Odd Birds*. Following his studies, he retained an unflagging curiosity about ancient Greece and has returned numerous times. *Menno in Athens* bridges two defining experiences in his life—his Anabaptist-Mennonite heritage and his love for Greece.

About the Illustrator

Lisa Rollo Kipp is a multimedia artist from Pelee Island, Ontario, whose love for art began at a very early age. The encouragement of her parents and a gifted high school teacher inspired her to continue her exploration of art. She currently enjoys oil painting, pen and ink drawing, and working with found items in nature.

Menno's Reading List

Aeschylus, *Prometheus Bound*. Trans. David Grene., in *Greek Tragedies*. Vol 1. Chicago: University of Chicago Press, 1969.

Anne Carson, *Fragments of Sappho*, in *If Not Winter*. New York: Random House, 2002.

Archilochus, Sappho, Alkman: Three Lyric Poets of the Seventh Century B.C., Trans. Guy Davenport. University of California Press, 1980.

Diogenes Laertius, *The Lives and Opinions of the Eminent Greek Philosophers*. Trans. Robert Drew Hicks. London: G. Bell & Sons, 1915.

Euripides, *The Trojan Women*. Trans. Richmond Lattimore, in *Greek Tragedies*. Vol 11. Chicago: University of Chicago Press, 1967.

Guthrie, W. K. C. *Socrates*. Cambridge: Cambridge University Press, 1971.

H. D. F. Kitto, *The Greeks*. London: Penguin, 1951.

Herodotus, *The Histories*. Trans. Aubrey de Selincourt. Penguin Books, Harmondsworth, 1971.

Hesiod, *Works and Days, Theogony*. Trans. Richmond Lattimore. Ann Arbor: University of Michigan Press, 1968.

Homer, *The Iliad*. Trans Richmond Lattimore. University of Chicago Press, 1951.

Michael Schmidt, *The First Poets*. New York: Knopf, 2005.

Pausanias, *Guide to Greece*, 2 Vols. Trans. Peter Levi. London: Penguin, 1971.

Plato, *Collected Dialogues*. Ed. Hamilton and Cairns. Princeton: Princeton University Press, 1961.

Plutarch, *Lives*. Trans. John Dryden. New York: Random House, 1864.

Robert Graves, *The Greek Myths*. London: Penguin, 1966.

Simone Weil, *Intimations of Christianity Among the Ancient Greeks*. London: Ark, 1987.

Simone Weil, *The Iliad, The Poem of Force*. Trans. Mary McCarthy. Wallingford: Pendle Hill, 1970.

Sophocles, *Antigone*. Trans. H. D. F. Kitto, in *Three Tragedies*. London: Oxford University Press, 1970.

The Odes of Pindar. Trans. C. M. Bowra. London: Penguin, 1969.

The Pythagoras Sourcebook. Trans. Kenneth Sylvan Guthrie. Grand Rapids: Phanes Press, 1988.

Thucydides, *The History of the Peloponnesian War*. Trans. Rex Warner. London: Penguin Books, 1968.

Ward, A.G. *The Quest for Theseus*. New York: Praeger, 1970.

Xenophon, *Memorabilia*. Trans. Henry Graham Dakyns. New York: Tandy-Thomas Company, 1909.

Notes

[1] Guy Davenport, *Archilochos, Sappho, Alkman*, 7-148.

[2] Diogenes Laertius, *Lives and Opinions of The Greek Philosophers*, Trans. Robert Drew Hicks.

[3] Menokritos stele inscription, Trans. E. M. Craik, *The Dorian Aegean*.

[4] Hippocrates, Vol II, 1923.

[5] Diogenes Laertius, Book 1, op. cit., 22-44.

[6] Ibid., 82-88.

[7] Ibid., 74-81.

[8] Simone Weil, *The Iliad or The Poem of Force*.

[9] K. S. Guthrie, *The Pythagorean Sourcebook and Library*.

[10] *The Odes of Pindar*, Trans. C. M. Bowra.

[11] Sophocles, *Antigone*, Trans. H. D. F. Kitto.

[12] Hesiod, *Theogony*, Trans. Richmond Lattimore.

[13] Diogenes Laertius, Book 1, op. cit., #s 68-74.

[14] A. G. Ward, *The Quest for Theseus*.

[15] *Greek Tragedies*, Vol 1, *Prometheus Bound*, Trans. David Grene.

[16] Thucydides, *The Peloponnesian War*, Trans. Rex Warner, Book 5, Chapters 84-116.

[17] Diogenes Laertius, Book 1, op. cit., 45-65.

[18] Euripides, *The Trojan Women*, in *Greek Tragedies*, Vol 11, Trans. Richmond Lattimore.

[19] W. H. C. Guthrie, *Socrates*.

Pandora Press is an independent publisher
focusing on scholarly and popular titles
in Anabaptist Mennonite Studies and beyond.

For a catalogue of recent publications, details for
submitting manuscripts, and contact information
please see our website: www.pandorapress.com

www.ingramcontent.com/pod-product-compliance
Lightning Source LLC
Chambersburg PA
CBHW031319160426
43196CB00007B/583